BULGARIA
THE LAND OF TREASURES

ATANAS ORACHEV
ANTONIY HANDJIYSKI

BULGARIA
THE LAND OF TREASURES

BORINA

First edition in Bulgaria, 2006
Borina Publishing House

E-mail: borina@borina.com
www.borina.com

ISBN 954-500-164-X

Printed in the Czech Republic

© Atanas Orachev, author, 2006
© Antoniy Handjiyski, author, 2006
© Vyara Kandjeva, photos
© Antoniy Handjiyski, photos
© Rosen Kolev, photos
© Antoniy Handjiyski, graphic design
© Vladimir Pomakov, translation
© BORINA Publishing House, Sofia
Bulgaria

CONTENTS

IN THE LAND OF TREASURES

In 1851, near the village Rozovets located in the Kazanlak valley, a certain grandfather Stoyan took out from a barrow a marble block. An opening gaped and precious antiques shined inside: even before Schliemann to excavate the Troy, the first Thracian treasure was discovered. It contained a gold wreath and things reminding those described by Homer in his epos: there, for the first time, the shining Thracian dinner sets and royal accoutrements were praised in song. In Bulgarian lands, the practice to lay precious metals in graves is older by three millennia than this was practiced in the times of the Trojan War. The earliest, from the end of the 5th millennium BC, are the gold findings at the village of Hotnitsa, the Varna and Dourankoulak necropolises. During the following three millennia, no gold objects have so far been found in Thrace. Such items appeared again only in the first centuries of the 1st millennium BC, from the time of which the cups found at town of Belene and the village Kazichene as well as in the Valchitran treasure most likely have come.

Gradually, in the museums had accumulated such a great amount of precious metals that the number of gold and silver objects as well as the 'underground treasuring' of coins formed the notion of Bulgaria as a peculiar 'country of treasures'. Of course, it is not the abundance of such items here that is important. Far more significant with respect to analyzing Thracian and, more generally speaking, the early European aristocratic culture, are the forms of the treasure objects and the scenes depicted on them.

Without the elegance of the long-neck rhytons and protomes of horses, bulls, Pegasus or sphinxes we could hardly imagine whatever royal dinner set. The same holds true for the rythonized pitchers and the short-neck rhytons: they are given the shape of 'female head' or protomes of deer, roe-deer, goat, ram, bull. The rhytonized amphorae are richly decorated with raised images. The little pitchers shine in gilt and the silver phials amaze the viewer.

The scenes depicted on the walls of these vessels as well as the applications on shields, armors and horse harnesses are diverse and show subjects not known to us from other sources. Attempts at interpreting them only on the basis of Hellenic mythology or by using complicated constructions related to the 'immortalization' of Thracian elite within the framework of an 'Orphic royal doctrine' are, as a rule, a failure. This is so because of the underestimation of their folklore aspect: these scenes reflect also the practices from Thracians' traditional ritualistic calendar.

Among the constant efforts and cares of the Hittite Kings, as early as in the 2nd millennium BC, was, first of all, to ensure the fertility of the cultivated fields and the well-being of the herds of domestic animals. Hittite texts reveal a series of rites aimed at *"ensuring rain"*, *"releasing the God-Sun from the prison"*, *"having the Big River letting free her flow"*… It was especially important to *"appease the wrath of Telepin"* who, when enraged: *"collects the grain, the Goddess of fields, the growth of plants, their blossoming and their swelling up with juices… cows, sheep and people stop leaving issue anymore… The mountain valleys dry up… The pastures dry up. The springs dry up. And famine settles in the country so that men and gods alike die of hunger."* Gods willingly fulfilled these ritual prayers: Kings were able to persuade them that the higher the number of people in the lands dependent on them and the more prosperous they are, the more precious donations the gods themselves were to receive.

Similar beliefs were traditional during the 1st millennium BC not only in Asia Minor and the Caucasus but also in the Balkans. Here they were typical for the largest European rural community in the antiquity, the Thracian one. The folklore simplicity of its rituality was so strong that its foundation had been well preserved in the course of the following two millennia. During the Middle Ages, it also became the essence of the beliefs of the new local animal-breeding community, the Bulgarians, not only because Thracians infused as a substantial component into the Bulgarian people.

Bulgarians continued successfully to develop the millennium-old rural Balkan traditions. It was exactly these traditions that let them to settle here soundly and to live, to shed sweat, tears and blood in the land of the key historical-geographic regions Mysia, Thrace and Macedonia in the course of the following thirteen centuries. Ancient-Thracian relics can be found in Bulgarian festival-ritualistic cycles of Koleda, Gergiovden, the 'kouker' plays and other ritual practices of seasonal nature, related to the everyday life of land tillers and settled animal-breeders. After 9th century AD, they are given a new meaning on a Christian basis in a number of Bulgarian cults like those of 'St. Marina', 'St. Iliya', 'St. Vlas', 'St. Modest', 'the Day of St. Trifon', 'the Day of St. Enyo (or the Summer St. John)', 'Babin Day'…

Beliefs in 'Dragons' and 'She-Dragons', 'sacred deer', 'samodiva', 'the weird sisters', and so on have a pagan nature, while many 'Services' are delivered on certain days in chapels dedicated to various saints. Such is the cult of the 'self-chased deer' that, on the appointed day and hour, comes and alone puts its head under the oblatory knife. The same is true for the successor of the 'Thracian Horseman', St. Georgi: in a syncretic image at folklore level it represents both the 'Hero-victor' and the 'knight' Krali Marko. Also, Bulgarian 'villi' and 'samovilli' (wood nymphs) coincide with the main characters of Thracian ritual cycles. The images and scenes from Thracian objects as if illustrate the local fairy tales and songs about 'Krali Marko', the 'Serpent-Dragon', the 'Three-headed Lamia', the 'Lower' and the 'Upper' worlds…

Almost every living thing in Thracian plots has also the ability to fly. Not birds alone fly. Horses and chariots are also winged. Wings are put on goats, deer and wolves/dogs. Lions are winged. Boars fly, too; griffons soar and sphinxes flap their wings; bulls also spread wings. Not only Thracian gods fly but so do the heroes. The tradition the heroes-younaks' (younak literally means 'a young, strong man') to be winged and able to fly has been preserved in Bulgarian folklore, too. Such abilities were given even to the Bulgarian voivode (literally means 'a leader in battles', 'military leader') from the second half of 19th century AD, Fillip Totyu about whom both Bulgarians and the Turks that chased him sincerely believed he was hiding wings under his shirt of a hero.

* * *

The earliest European worked gold has been found in Bulgarian lands. The first gold anthropomorphic and zoomorphic applications, rings, ringlets and beads that people started to bury in the Mother-Earth are dated from before seven millennia. Beliefs and mythological cycles about anthropomorphic goddesses and gods took shape; at those times again and in the same lands scepters were made that symbolize the royal power.

The brilliant pre-historic Chalkolithic cultures were wiped out in the 4th millennium BC by a complex of factors, among which the grand climatic changes stand out followed by the invasion of Nordic peoples: they began rushing into the Balkans in the last centuries of the millennium. During the following two millennia here formed the first big Balkan community, the Thracian one. It covered the vast region from the northern ranges of the Carpathian Mountains in the north to the White (Aegean) Sea in the south; to the south-west it bordered to the Adriatic Coast; to the north-west Thracian lands bordered with the lands of the German tribe Suevs, while to the north-east the border entered into today's Ukrainian steppes that divide the Thracian from the Scythian community. That is why to Dionysos Periegetes Thracians possessed an "endless land" (Dion. Per. 323) and according to the 'father of history' Herodotos (5.3) *"Thracians are, along with Indians, the most populous people on the face of the Earth."*

The totality of data points out that by the 1st millennium BC Thracians had already formed about 90 different communities, which we provisionally call 'tribes'. From the 4th century BC on, part of these tribes had united under the scepter of the Kings of the Odryses dynasty founded by Teres I. During the centuries that followed, the Kings of this dynasty began to pile up treasures of artfully made objects. They were made by toreuts of different origin but work for and servicing exactly the Thracian royal economy.

To bury precious metal outside the necropolises became a stable practice exactly from the end of 6th - 5th centuries BC on. The first such treasures consists of silver coins of great nominal value, from the south-west Thracian tribes. The picture changes by the end of the 5th century BC and becomes typical for the whole of the 4th century BC. Then, apart from purely coin-containing findings people had begun to hide in the earth objects made of precious metal, too. The following more important things can be said with responsibility about the Thracian aristocratic practice to keep in the earth treasures as well as to put inside tombs valuable objects:

1. The valuable objects from before the middle of the 4th century BC are, as a rule, an inseparable part of the Odryses' royal economy. Typical features of this economy was the strict regulation of contacts with

the outside world, the supreme ownership of Odryses' royal family of all that is over and under the earth as well as the ways of collecting taxes, duties, charges and donations. Because of that (but also because of a number of other factors and most of all because of the stern control over extraction of gold and silver) until the middle of the 4th century BC only Odryses from the highest standing families were allowed to hoard treasures. However, they did not bury them in the earth: part of them they put in their tombs but another part (and the bigger one at that) was hoarded in the royal treasury. After Phillip II the Macedon occupied the key areas in the kingdom of Kersebleptes in 341-340 BC, he also captured the Odryses' treasury; it was most likely kept in the 'Holy Fortress' located in the 'Holy Mountain' (today's Tekir Dag in Turkey). As a result, a lot of vessels from Odryses' royal dinner sets popped up in burial and treasure findings to the north of Haemos (Stara Planina Range) as well.

2. The number of treasure objects found to the north of Stara Plainina Range exceed by many times the findings from the lands to the south of it. The ratio is 10 to 1 and it comes to point at the exclusive nature of 'Mysian' as compared to 'Thracian' findings. This fact cannot be explained only by the 'diplomatic activity' of the Odryses' King Kotys I (around 383-360 BC) in the land of Triballs and Gettae: the articles found in the lands of the Lower Danube that can be ascribed with certainty to Odryses are more than abundant. The information supplied by the historian Thucydides that, in contrast to Persian the Odryses' Kings *"followed a tradition… more to take than to give"* is contrary to the above explanation.

3. In the 4th century BC, when most treasures were buried, the building of monumental Thracian tombs and under-barrow complexes flourished. There, along with the dead who at those times might not have been members of the Odryses elite, the practice of placing gold and silver objects of exceptional value had started.

4. The practice of rich Thracian burials from the second half of the 4th century BC on is not such an exceptional phenomenon. It makes a very strong impression only when compared to the Hellenic traditions. It is indicative that exactly in the Persian kingdom, conquered by the troops of Alexander III the Great one can find good parallels both with Thracian tombs and with burial donations. It is a known

fact that in the 30 000-, 32 000- or 40 000-strong army led by the Macedonian King in 334 BC to conquer the world there were 5000 to 7000 Thracians. This comes to say that they were among the most numerous draft in the army and part of these Odryses, Triballes and Agrianes elite that 'had seen the world around' while being soldiers of Alexander, returned later to their homeland.

5. In any case, the master-toreuts were of various origins. Within the borders of the Odryses' royal economy they got a higher prestige than their peers in Hellenic police-states where a considerable part of them were meteks and even slaves. In Thrace the craftsmen were privileged and part of the entourage of the royal institute. This higher public status and authority seems to have permitted them to re-create more freely on local grounds and for the royal needs the images and the ideas that have come from the Anatolian-Caucasian, from Persian, from Hellenic and, from the end of the 5th century BC, also from the Phoenician toreutic schools.

6. It became fashionable to see in the scenes from the treasures 'Thracian mystery practices', which allegedly were related to the royal ideology of 'immortalization'. These interpretations are artful but they are beneath criticism. Herodotos was the first to point out that the 'secret' of the local mysteries was known only to the 'initiates': how then and from where such scenes had been depicted by the toreuts? To accept these scenes for 'mystery practices' related to the 'immortalization' of Thracian elite would mean first, that craftsmen who created these objects should also have been 'initiated in the mysteries' and this is an absurd assumption having in mind exactly the postulated strictly aristocratic nature of the 'occult Thracian Orphism'. Then, also both the craftsmen and the respective client would have broken their 'secret', and we know quite well that the initiated ones took a special oath to keep this 'secret'.

7. Phillip II the Macedon, Alexander III the Great and Lysimachos in the second half of the 4th century BC destroyed the until then Odryses' monopoly on everything and everybody in Thrace. The newly emerged political, economic and cultural relations had allowed a considerably larger part of the Thracian elite of those times to hoard treasures.

8. During the 'Hellenistic epoch' treasures were hoarded both in

coins and in precious objects and the inflow of coins of gold and silver had definitely increased. The increase of this flow of coins was based on those factors thanks to which the production underwent expansion and trade was freed from the rather strict regulation. The increased demand for mercenaries also played an additional role in boosting economy: Thracians regularly joined the armies of Hellenistic rulers. All that allowed many other members of Thracian elite to adopt the practice of hoarding treasures, to build monumental tombs and to lay valuables in them, something that, until then, was exclusively an Odryses' practice.

9. Since the 3rd and until the 1st centuries BC coin findings predominate. The treasure articles are not only less in number, quantity and weight but have lost their brilliance and impressiveness. This fact was not due to some kind of 'Thracian toreuts' leaving for the Scythian lands under the 'pressure of Celts'. A new, 'Hellenistic epoch' had been settling, which caused changes in the way of thinking, of values and mind-settings, in fashions; a decisive blow was also delivered to the Odryses' royal economy. In fact, craftsmen did not flee but rather the royal orders decreased and the practice to collect those brilliant 'gifts' typical for the former royal dinner sets simply stopped. It was exactly that the prestigious vessels were the first to disappear: making of rhytons stopped, there were no more the richly decorated rhytonized amphorae, one could not see anymore little pitchers, there were no exquisite royal phials.

10. Many and most varying explanations have been and are being offered on the practice to bury treasures. For the time being, the complex analysis outlines the observation that Thracian culture as any rural culture was able to deal in money and gold affairs only in the case the town culture served as its middleman. This explanation is simple and that's why it seems convincing: gold, even when it is in an unbelievable abundance, when appears in Thracian community structured under the total King's aegis and variegated occasionally by privileged artisan-trader's communes, cannot 'contribute' in a sustained way to the prosperity of the local economy. It seems one of the reasons that had led to burying of precious metal in the earth has its roots in this conjecture. I.e. this has been a practice not because of and not for some immediate danger. This obser-

vation, along all the other, allows also for understanding why in the indisputably poorer and not so well developed part of Ancient Thrace as was the Lower Danube plain, treasure consisting of precious objects and coins occur ten times more frequently.

* * *

This edition presents treasure articles the selection of which was determined not by the brilliance and weight of the precious metal but by the striving to illustrate the basic in the ancient-Thracian beliefs. The reader should bear in mind that local lands, in which people buries treasure for millennia on end, offer those favourable factors, which allow for early development of all aspects of man's economic activity. Among these is also the first European metallurgy and metal working. The sacral dimensions of the earliest in Europe worked gold impress as do the first European scepter, symbol of the royal power as well as the first manifestations, if not of letters, then at least of proto-letters as early as by the end of the 5th millennium BC.

This millennia-old background outlines the European significance of Bulgarian lands: here, the foundations of at least a part of the beginnings of the European civilization models were laid along with the taking of form of the principles on the basis of which two independent structures, the 'rural' and the 'urban' ones, have differentiated and developed. Nowhere else in Europe, the researcher would have a better field to follow up the peculiarity and to outline the essential differences between the rural and the urban culture. To perceive the principle differences in the outlook on life, to view in detail the difference in the everyday stereotypes and the ways by which both peasants and town people perceive, give a philosophical meaning and strive to organize the world. To understand that the best of all times have been present here when the two cultures had cooperated but when they started to counteract in a violent way, the destruction and anarchy settled in the Balkans.

"In the history of civilizations as well as in the history of personalities the childhood is decisive" wrote the French historian Jacque le Goff. The European 'aristocratic childhood' has its roots in the Balkans too, and Thracian monuments illustrate a part of its initial stages.

THE TREASURE OF VALCHITRAN

This treasure was found quite accidentally in 1924, while farmers were doing a deep plough of a vineyard near the village Valchitran (District of Pleven). After vicissitudes (a part of the precious things that were found in the beginning were later cut into pieces during a sharing, while another part simply 'disappeared') only 13 vessels, all weighing a total of 12 425 g got into then People's Museum in Sofia: a big kantharos-like vessel, tri-section vessel, a big and three smaller chalices each one with a single handle, two big and five smaller disks. Apart from gold, electron (an alloy of gold and silver) was also used in their making, and what is the most intriguing, amber. In making the disk decoration, with bulbous handles, makers of the vessels used the technique 'niello': a rarely occurring inlay of silver on gold.

The man who first published information on this treasure, doctor Vasil Mikov, has done a comparative analysis and gives the most acceptable dating: 9th – 8th century BC. Of late, because of uncertain parallels with the treasure from Bessarabia and some other data, it has been ac-

cepted that the most likely dating of the Valchitran treasure is from 13th century BC.

So far, apart from the Valchitran treasure two more cups from Thracian lands are also known: one is from Belene (a small town on the Danube riverside) and one is from Kazichene (a village in Sofia plain, now a borough of Sofia City). Both are made of gold; they definitely are not from the Chalcolithic period and precede the initial stages of ancient Greek colonization of Thrace in 8th – 7th centuries BC. It seems certain that the big, wide and relatively deep gold vessels were used to dilute and mix wine: the ancients used to mix wine, honey and milk in them when they were about to make effusions in honor of Dionysos, and maybe this holy triad corresponds to Homer's 'kykeion'. In any case, these were the sacred liquids, acquired in a miraculous way by the maenads, as described in Euripides: *"One of them grabbed the thyrsos and hit the rock: a jet of crystal clear water spurted from it; another threw the thyrsos on the ground and to her God sent a spring of wine. Those that wanted to drink a white drink raked up the earth with the tips of* their fingers and found streams of milk; and from the ivy of the thyrsi sweet honey run down."

The vessels have a good parallels in Homer (Od. 9. 196-211): "*I had with myself a goat bag full of dark sweet wine given to me by Maron, son of Evanteos, priest of Apollo, protector of Ismaros… He offered me wonderful gifts, gave me 7 talents of beautifully worked gold, also gave me a crater – a whole of it made of silver, then he poured in all twelve amphorae sweet unmixed wine, a divine drink*". Production of sweet wine in Thrace is also confirmed by Atheneos (Dipnosoph. 1.31a): "*Epicharmos* [of Cicily, author of comedies, lived in 6th – 5th century BC] *states that the Bibline wine has been called so because of some mountain named Biblina. And Armenidas says that Biblina is a region in Thrace* [between the mouths of the rivers Stryma and Mesta], *which has also been called Antisara and Oisyme. Thrace, and generally speaking, the lands adjacent to it, have been justly considered the lands where sweet wine is made.*" The 'chalice' Priam gave to Achiles to ransom the body of the dead Hector (Hom.II. 24.228-234): "*Priam opened the nice lids of the chests. He took out of them … also a beautiful chalice, a thing of great value, which Thracian men* had given to Priam as a present when he had visited them as an emissary."

It is accepted that data on Thrace presented by Homer should be dated as far back as from the late Bronze Age. This, however, is disputable: the only certain date, which can be accepted as a terminus antequem is 6th century BC (it was then that Homer's epos had been edited for the last time). There are indeed rich cultures of the late Bronze Age in Thrace but gold findings dated for certain from that Age have not yet been found, though metalworking here had been quite well developed. An information was released of late about a "silver treasure" from the "Bronze Age": the disputable finding does not contradict this observation and if the dating is correct, then the question is to what extent the precious metal (along with iron, which at those times was 14 times as expensive as gold) in that Age was not an exceptional 'royal prerogative', inaccessible (not allowed) not only to the common people but also to its noble elite. Some gold findings from today's Bessarabia, provisionally dated from the late Bronze Age do not belittle but even exalt this observation.

The Valchitran Treasure
Gold. Treasure, Valchitran (District of Pleven); 13 pieces of total weight 12 500 g.
14th – 13th or 9th – 8th centuries BC. It consists of large kantahros-like vessel, tri-section vessel, a large and

three smaller chalices, each with a single handle, two big and five little disks. Along with the disks, which have bulbous-shaped handles because of the

'niello' technique, the making of the big kantharos-like vessel with two handles also impresses. It is 22.4 cm high and weighs 4395 g. Made of two parts soldered together with silver and its two handles are supplied with spigots, coming out of the mouth and nailed with gold tacks.

The Valchitran Treasure
Gold. Treasure, Valchitran
(District of Pleven);
14th – 13th or 9th – 8th centuries
BC

Big 'lid' *(or kymbal, "κνμβαλον")*
diameter 37 cm, weight 1775 g.
Its outer side is covered with geometric
helical ornaments executed in 'niello'
technique (silver bands stuck on the
body of the vessel and having their
rims dotted). On the inside the handle
is padded with bronze pad laid on a
massive bronze circle with a cross in
the middle.

A big and three little chalices
The chalices are of the kyathos type;
the big one is 12.3-cm high and weighs
919 g; the three little ones (one is 8.9-
cm high and weighs 132 g; the other
two are 8.2-cm high, weighing 130 g
each). Made by the same technique as
the kantharos-like vessel.

Tri-section vessel
23.9-cm long, 5.3-cm high, weigh
1190 g
Consists of leaf-like 'pools' connected
to each other by slightly curbed tubes
of 'white gold' (electron).

18 |

THE ODRYSES' ROYAL NECROPOLIS NEAR DOUVANLII

The big ritual-funeral complex found near the village Douvanlii (District of Plovdiv) consists of 29 individual, well-seen in the countryside area barrows dated from 6th to 1st centuries BC. Of all these only five: Moushovitsa Mogila (i.e. 'barrow'), Koukova Mogila, Golyamata (Big) Mogila, Bashova Mogila and Arabadzhiyska Mogila – are rich of artifacts.

Treasure objects found there are listed in an article by Prof. Bogdan Filov: the findings from the necropolis and the known in that time precious things from Ancient Thrace had allowed the great Bulgarian archaeologist to state in a special publication that the postulates on 'Scythian bestial' style should be revised and that it is necessary to investigate the existence of a Thracian toreutic school. Bogdan Filov connects the necropolis with Thracian Bessi, while the analyses made by Prof. Margarita Tacheva allow researchers to comprehend that the necropolis belonged to Odryses' royal dynasty.

Some of the treasure objects found there and dated 6th – 5th centuries BC have their parallels in Homer. Here are for instance the descriptions in Can. 10 of the 'Iliad': *"Among Trojans there was someone called Dolon, son of Eumedeos, the heavenly herold, rich in gold and copper… Spare my life and I will give you ransom because in my home there is copper, and gold and well-wrought iron. Of all those things my father would give you willingly countless ransom, had he knew I am alive in Achaean ships… So, if you wish to get into Trojan bivouac, there at the side are the recently arrived Thracians, they have pitched their camp farthest of all, at the very end; among them is King Rhesos, son of Eioneos. I saw his horses, the most beautiful and stoutest, whiter than the snow, racing as fast as the wind. His chariot is nicely decorated with gold and silver. He came with weapons, made of gold, huge, marvelous to look at; it does not become mortal men to wear them but gods immortal…"*

Similar to the above are the descriptions in Euripides tragedy "Rhesos", which does not belong to his pen and was written some time by the end of 5th – the beginning of the 4th century BC:

"… like a torrent flowed hither the Thracian army. Seized by fear we rushed the herds towards the summits of the mountain, lest some Argivian may come hither led by his lust for loot and to put your sheeppens to destruction. But when non-Hellenic words reached our ears, our fear disappeared; then I approached the King's scouts on the road and asked them in Thracian language who was their leader and whose son was that who, being an ally of the Priamids has set off for the town. And when I heard everything I wanted to know, I stood still and saw King Rhesos like a God, standing upright in his chariot pulled by Thracian horses. Golden harness weighed down on the necks of his horses, whiter than snow and his shield plated in gold, was shining on his body. Gorgons made of copper and affixed on horses' frontlets, as if had come from the aegis of Goddess Athena stroke terror by the ringing of their many bells."

Definitely, these descriptions have no parallels with materials from the late Bronze Age in Thrace. On the other hand almost everything described above can be seen in the articles found in the Odryses' royal necropolis, including the applications of the Gorgon-Medusa. Gold breastplates, gold rings and adornments, gold and silver (gilded) decorations on armors of Thracian Kings, ornamentations on chariots, shields and horse harness of the heavy armored aristocratic elite become something quite usual for Thrace exactly since 6th century BC on.

In the early materials from the necropolis one can perceive a strong Iranian influence, which shows in many "Ahemenid" by their typology and ornamentation early objects from the necropolis. Their character made Prof. M. Tacheva to even see in part of them the funereal stock of an unknown 'Persian princess'. However, here some findings were revealed of doubtlessly Odryses' character and there is no way they to have been made not in local workshops which, even if they were not royal ones, had carried out royal orders. Such for instance are the typical silver kantharos-like vessels, the handles of which are crossed by massive metal bands. They served to wind around them ivy as can be seen on some of the kantharos-like vessels on Abdera coins from the first quarter of 4th century BC.

Amphora
*Silver with gilt. Koukova Mogila at
the Odryses' royal necropolis near
village Douvanlii; height 27 cm,
weight 1344 g.
End of the 4th century BC.
The neck of this amphora is separated
from the spherical body by a band of
ovulae, and has a 27-leaf rosette on
its bottom. Handles are shaped like
monsters with lion heads turned backwards. They have pointed ears and big*

*screwed horns, broken at one of the
monsters. Their shoulders are stylized like the figure of eight, while
their tails end with their tufts of
hairs arranged in a fan-shaped way.
Their forelegs are tri-dimensional,
their muscles are stylized like lotus
blossom, while their ribs are given
the shape of slightly curved palmettos. The hind legs are set on a high
tambour. On one of the handles there
is a spout for pouring out the liquid.*

Phial

Silver with gilt. Bashova Mogila at the Odryses' royal necropoluis near village of Douvanlii; height 3 cm, dia. 20.5 cm, weight 428 g.

Third quarter of the 5th century BC.

On the inside of the phial there are four quadrigas engraved in gold, swiftly fleeing, with a driver and a warrior on each quadriga. The drivers wear long chitons (only one has a mantle thrown on his shoulders), while the warriors are fully accoutred: helmets, chain-mails, greaves and shields. Two of them wear Chalkidikian, the third wears Corinthian and the fourth, Thracian type of helmet. The round shields are decorated with a horse, lion and centaurs. It is generally accepted that on this phial a scene from the "agon dur-ing the Panathénées" dedicated to the victory of Goddess Athena in the gigantomachia is presented. During the contest the 'apobaths' came down and climbed repeatedly on chariots. Howev-er, the way of representing the contests with chariots in the Kazanlak tomb and a number of other considerations suggest a Thracian agonal character of the scene. It is indicative that the war-riors are shown in various stands: one is about to jump, two of them have stepped on the chariot axis, and only the warrior wearing the Thracian type of helmet stands firmly on his two legs on the floor of the chariot. The scene suggests the Odryses' royal order, where in a race with chariots the most likely winner is the Thracian team.

Cylix from a dinner set of the Odryses' Kings

Silver with gilt. Bashova Mogila at the Odryses' royal necropolis near the village Douvanliy; height 3 cm, diameter 13 cm, weight 220 g. Third quarter of the 5th century BC. On the bottom of this vessel, in a gold frame of laurel leaves the image of a goddess is engraved. She wears a peplos on a short mantle and rides an 'Amazonian' horse, drifting over a sea, in which fishes swim. On the outer, undecorated side of this cylix, there is an inscription hammered out in Greek letters that reads ΔΑΔΑΛΕΜΕ (Da dale me), of likely translation from Thracian: "Mother Earth, help!"

Applications for armor

Silver. The Big Mogila at the Odryses'
royal necropolis near the village
Douvanliy (District of Plovdiv); height
6.5 cm.
About the middle of the 5ᵗʰ century
BC.
Three of the applications with Nike's
image (made on different matrices)
have been found together with five
applications of lion and Gorgon: they
form a complete suite for armor. What
impresses also is the non-Hellenistic
appearance of the Gorgon: it does not
instil fear being definitely depicted
smiling and looks rather a good-
natured than striking horror monster.

Little pitcher
Silver. Bashova Mogila at the Odryses'
royal necropolis near the village
Douvanliy; height 8.6 cm, max.
diameter 8.3 cm, weight 236 g.
Second half of the 5th century BC.
The body of this little pitcher is covered
by flutes. On its mouth shows an
inscription in Thracian language
with Greek letters ΔΑΔΑΛΕΜΕ
(Da dale me), with likely translation
from Thracian "Mother Earth help!"
but because of the Alanian-Ossetian
"dada" another meaning is not less
possible, namely "Smash (them) or
repulse (the evil forces), Father!"
(Dada leme). This inscription occurs
also on other vessels from royal dinner
sets and can be accepted as typical for
the Odryses. That is why it cannot be
found on vessels manufactured after
340 BC.

Rhyton with a horse protome
Silver with gilt. Bashova Mogila at
the Odryses' royal necropolis near the
village Douvanliy; height 20.6 cm,
weight 400 g.
Third quarter of the 5th century BC.
The mouth of one of the finest rhytons
found in Thrace is covered with pearls
and ovulae and under it an elegant
frieze of alternating lotus blossoms
and palmettos linked by volutes are
engraved. The body of the rhyton is
covered with decoration of vertical
tongue-like flutes, which end in its

lower part, shaped like horse protome:
the flutes are separated from the
protome by a girdle of pearls. The
horse breast band, mane and hooves
are gilded. The opening for drinking
is installed on the horse breast. On
the inside of the rhyton an inscription
shows in Thracian language with
Greek letters ΔΑΔΑΛΕΜΕ. It could
be read as "Da dale me" with likely
translation from Thracian as "Mother
Earth, help!" or "Dada leme" meaning
"Smash or repulse (the evil forces),
Father!"

Kantharos

Silver with gilt. The Big Mogila at the Odryses' royal necropolis near the village Douvanliy; height 25.5 cm, weight 1073 g.

Around the middle of 5th century BC. This kantharos has a tall stem and highly set, curbed handles, which come out of the mouth: to it (above the handles) the artisan has soldered on each side a silver head of a Sylen adorned with a wreath of ivy. Scenes with abundant gilt are engraved on the vessel walls. One of these shows Dionysos moving to the left with a Maenad walking against him and carrying in her arms a roe-deer fawn. This scene has a good parallel in the tragedy "Maenads" by Euripides where the suite of Agava, the daughter of founder of Thebes, Kadmes, is described: "But then other of them, who were recently given birth and their breasts were full because they had left their children, took in arms fawns or wild wolf-cubs and suckled them with white milk." On the other side of the kantharos a Satyr and a Maenad holding a thyrsos in her hand are depicted. The naked Satyr has the skin of sacrificed roe-deer thrown upon his shoulders and holds a thyrsos in his right hand. These scenes illustrate rites from the cycle of Dionysos.

THE ROGOZEN TREASURE

This treasure was found in the centre of the village Rogozen, District of Vratsa, in two separate parts and contains 108 phials, 54 pitchers, 2 cups and 1 scyphos. There total weight is 19.91 kg. One hundred and thirty-one of these vessels have gilt on them. There are many hypotheses on the origin, amassing and the reason to have this treasure buried where it was found. The nature of the treasure and the pattern of events as known to us allow for making the following definite observations to be made:

- inscriptions on the neck place 13 of the vessels as property of the Odryses' King Kotys I (around 383-360 BC) and his successor Kersebleptes (359-340 BC). These vessels have undoubted parallels in findings from the Mogilanska Mogila, Alexandrovo, Borovo and Adzhigyol, where on four phials and 3 rhytons the name of Kotys I can be read;

- in an inscription on the mouth of a vessel the name Satokos can also be read; there is only one Satok whose name may stand on a vessel like that: Prince Satokos/Sadokos, son of Sitalkes (431-429 BC). On the mouth there is another inscription: "Kotys, son of Apollo";

- the second name from the inscriptions on vessels' necks is that of settlements where they were manufactured (formulas "To the man named so-and-so, from there-and-there" and "Made/assembled by so-and-so to so-and-so" – ΔΙΣΛΟΙΑΣ ΕΠΟΙΗΣΕ ΚΟΤΥΟΣ ΕΓ ΒΕΟ meaning "Disloy made/assembled to Kotys, from Beo";

- according to inscriptions, workshops in Apri, Beo, Argiske/Ergiske, Geysti and Saythaba worked for the Kings of Odryses. It is disputable whether these settlements were at the same time residences of Odryses' royal families but more than likely they were privileged communes of the kind the 'emporium' Pistiros near the village Vetren (District of Pazardzhik). The most important of these communes was Beo: its central settlement was located by the 'Diagonal Road' from Central Europe to Asia Minor and, judging from the periplus by Pseudo Skylax from Kariadna, corresponds to the town of Peo(n);

- Rogozen vessels have no parallels in burials in the necropolis at Douvanliy and the findings from villages Daskal Atanasovo and Dalboki dated the end of the

6th to the third quarter of the 5th centuries BC;

- The treasure contains only pitchers, phials and cups and lacks the typical for other treasures collection of vessels, components of parade armaments and applications for horse harness. Therefore, it can be assumed that this is a part of a treasure, which has been shared: the fact that the value of the vessels is equivalent to 4000 Athenean drachmas (silver equivalent).

It is a known fact that, after the death of Kotys in 360 BC, the Macedonian aggression into Thrace had started. In 340 BC Hieron Teichos was captured and most likely it was there that the royal treasury was kept. Shortly after that Philip II the Macedon was called to help the Scythian King Ateas who had some accounts to square with the Triballs. In the summer of 339 BC, he set off for today's Dobrudzha taking along part of the Odryses' treasury. Ateas, however, refused the aid from the Macedonians and finally it came to an overt conflict in which the superannuated Scythian King was killed. Phillip set off for Macedonia crossing the lands of Triballs who demanded from him a share of the loot. The Macedonian King underestimated there military power and turned down their demand. In the battled that ensued Phillip was wounded and became lame for the rest of his life, while Triballs took away the Macedonian supply train. According to the practice of those times, the loot was shared. The map of the certain (inscribed) vessels from Odryses' treasury outline territories encompassing almost the whole of today's North Bulgaria, and also Adzhigyol to Krayova (Romania) and the region of Iron Gates (Serbia). It is quite possible that some of the Odryses' vessels (from Adzhigyol for instance?) to have been donated by Phillip II himself, who carried with himself a part of the Odryses' treasury.

Two shares of the Odryses' treasure fell into the hands of a Triball ruler who buried them: most likely during Alexander III the Great campaign against the Tribal King Syrmos, which took place in 334 BC. In this way, the chronological limits within which the Rogozen treasure was amassed seem to have been the last decades of the 5th century BC and 339 BC. The inception date of amassing (save the disputable name of Sadok) could be determined at least from the Rogozen phial with "two labryses", which undoubtedly are a royal symbol of the Odryses' King Medokos or of Amadokos the Old.

Pitcher from a dinner set of Odryses' Kings

Silver. Treasure, the village Rogozen (District of Vratsa), height 11.5 cm, max. diameter of the body 8 cm, weight 127.2 g.

End of the 5th century BC.

The body of the pitcher is divided into two disproportionate belts by a band (notches of dots). Central position on the wider belt occupies the winged goddess. She is erect, with disproportionately large head and a long chiton falling down to her heels, flung across her left shoulder and passing under her right armpit. In both her hands she holds a dog whose head is turned backwards. Two winged centaurs with their heads turned full face gallop towards her.

A bull is depicted on the lower frieze, attacked by four enraged dogs, two on each side of the bull. The bull, dogs and centaurs (griffons, sphinxes) in combination with the Great Goddess seem to be a Thracian subject-matter because in Hellas (also with Persian Artemis) the sacred animals are the dog, the deer and the lion). It is possible in this particular case to have a Thracian version of the Hellenized subject-matter on the Maenad Agava and her 'swift dogs' presented. If that is so, then the centaurs have replaced 'those men' from Euripides drama "Maenads" who wanted to catch the daughter of Thebes founder, the Phoenician Kadmes and mother of the Thebes King Pentheos.

**Pitcher from Odryses Kings'
dinner set**
Silver with gilt. Treasure, the village
Rogozen (District of Vratsa), height
13.5 cm, max. diameter of the body 8.5
cm, weight 234.9 g.
First half of the 4th century BC.
The body of the pitcher is girdled by
a frieze with figurines on it. There
is a mirror-image of the bare-footed
Thracian Goddess-Virgin, which is
mounted on a large cat (panther or
mountain lion, also called 'bars') in a
lady's (Amazonian) manner in a quiet
pace moving to the right. In her right
hand she holds a bow and an arrow
that personify her, while with her left
arm she hugs the animal. She is clad
in a long, falling down to her heels
short-sleeved-chiton (thrown on her
left shoulder and passing across to her
right armpit), and her head turned full
face (the so-called Thracian manner)
looks majestically at the onlookers.
Her hair is braided and the braids fall
freely down by her face. Between the
two images of the Goddess the peculiar
Thracian scene 'a lion attacks a deer'
is shown. The deer is a fallow deer as
may be deducted from its antlers. It
seems that to Thracians the 'Golden'
or the 'Self-chased' deer is most
frequently presented as a fallow deer.

Pitcher from the Odryses Kings' dinner set

Silver. Treasure, the village Rogozen (District of Vratsa); height 12 cm, max. diameter of the body 8.3 cm, weight 134.8 g.
The first half of the 4th century BC. The frieze with figurines is of a remarkably high relief and represents two winged quadrigas – two-wheeled carriages of hanging chassis and seats set opposite to each other. The winged horses stand upright on their hind legs and this scene shows well the craftsmanship of the Thracian artisan: the horses as if play a horo (Bulgarian folk chain-dance). One of the carriages is steered by the Great Goddess behind which sits the Thracian Goddess-Virgin holding a bow in her left hand. In the other chariot the roles are changed: the Goddess-Virgin steers the chariot, while the Great Goddess holds in her hand a budding twig with seven branches. Most likely these scenes depict two of the most important ritual cycles in Thrace, which correspond to the 'sourvakar' (today the New Year) and 'kouker' (today the Easter) games: in a wider context this corresponds to the winter and spring cycles respectively.

Pitcher from the Odryses Kings' dinner set

Silver with gilt. Treasure, the village Rogozen (District of Vratsa); height 13.5 cm, max. diameter of the body 8.5 cm, weight 134.3 g.
End of 5th – the first half of 4th centuries BC
This vessel has a pear-like shape, its handle is missing and its bottom turns into a low conical foot decorated with a ring of ovulae. The shoulders of the pitcher are girdled in a kind of wreath of 13 ram's heads (equal to the number of months according to the Lunar calendar?), while below this wreath is a frieze depicting a procession of animals. In its centre is the Great Goddess in full face. She 'comes out' from the wings of a lion-griffon whose tail ends up with a serpent's head. A panther (or leopard) is rushing towards the hind of the griffon and

under the latter two deer run to the left. In front of the griffon's head there is a raptor with an 'iron beak', which has bitten a snake's head. From left to right on the central scene there are two fantastic-looking animals: the left one has lion legs, a tail ending in a serpent's head and on its back, with a goat protome looking to the right, towards the griffon; the figure behind the central griffon belongs to a winged hoofed animal (Pegasos?), under it a bare human foot shows and above it one can see human hand holding a knife. The expert in art Ivan Marazov interprets this picture as a 'Thracian version of the battle of Bellerophon' with the Chimera. The frieze presents a Thracian mythical-ritualistic scene related to the Great Thracian Goddess, while the fantastic-looking animals have their parallels in the epos of Ossetinians.

**Pitcher from the Odryses Kings'
dinner set**

Silver with gilt. Treasure, the village
Rogozen (District of Vratsa); height 14.3
cm, max. diameter of the body 7.5 cm,
weight 128 g.
End of 5th – the first half of 4th
centuries BC
It has been accepted that the frieze on
this pitcher presents the 'ninth exploit of
Hercules' – his battle with the Amazon
Hippolyta. The hero is a young man,
without a stitch on, holding a kind of
shepherd's crook in his right hand; while
with his left hand he is trying to deliver
a blow into the groins of the Amazon
swooping down on him. The heroine
is clad in a dress reaching down to her

knees and has undoubtedly disarmed
her adversary holding a spear in her
hands which rests on his head. The
Goddess, because this is not Hippolyta
but the Thracian Goddess-Virgin is
accompanied on the right side by a
protome of a lion-griffon, and on her left
side, by a 'horse head'. This Thracian
mythological scene has no parallels in the
Hellenistic iconography and the motif of
'accompanying heads' has its parity in
the scenes on the treasure from Letnitsa.
In this particular case there are two such
parities which correspond to what we
know about the practices of the Hittite's
Gods and Kings who used to have two
advisers: one sitting on the left side and
the other, on the right.

***A gobele from the Odryses Kings'
dinner set***

*Silver with gilt. Treasure, the village
Rogozen (District of Vratsa); height
20 cm, diameter of the mouth 13 cm,
weight 316.2 g.
End of 5th – the first half of 4th
centuries BC*
*Bi-conical goblet of large proportions,
hammered out on a matrix from a thin
silver leaf. Images on it are raised and
details of the decoration, chiselled.
Under the mouth of the goblet there is
a frieze composed of deer antlers the
forks of which gradually change into
little bird heads (in the Ossetinian
epos the cart-rails of the richer nartas
(sleds) are made of deer antlers). The
central frieze presents a procession of
a goat, deer, two other deer (depicted
in parallel?) and a raptor. The goat
(under the form of which Thracian
Dionysos used to appear among men)*
*is presented as moving to the right,
before the raptor. It has three little
winglets and his horns are powerfully
curved backwards. It seems that the
'eight-legged' deer leads the strange
procession moving to the right and it
also has a small winglet on its chest –
unfortunately its head is missing (this
part of the vessel has been chopped
off during deep plough of the field).
Especially impressive is the raptor: it is
presented half-face, has a curved beak
and a large horn on its head. It holds
a fish in its beak (taken by the mouth),
while its talons have clutched around
a hare. Similar birds with 'iron beaks'
(falcons and eagles along with 'iron
stallion' and wolf with an iron snout')
are also known from 'Nartian epos'.
On the bottom of the goblet there is a
scene presenting 'wolf/dog attacking a
wild boar'.*

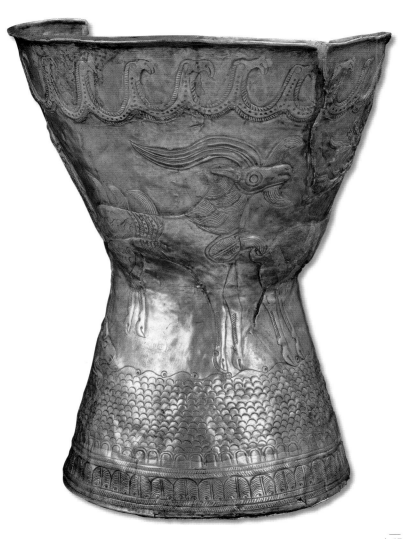

Phial from the Odryses Kings' dinner set
Silver with gilt. Treasure, the village Rogozen (District of Vratsa); height 4.5 cm, diameter 11.6 cm, weight 104.8 g.
Before 339 BC.
Around the umbo of the phial, which is of the type of a dish, an ornamental frieze has been formed consisting of eight plastic almonds. They alternate with relatively coarsely stylized lotus blossoms. Above it there is another frieze consisting of eight carefully made heads separated by lotus blossoms. The heads are entirely identical, have expressive eyes and small lips; their hair is plaited and braids fall freely down along both sides of their faces. The iconographic type coincides with those pitchers from the Treasure of Rogozen on which the Great Goddess is depicted.

Phial from the Odryses Kings' dinner set

Silver with gilt. Treasure, the village Rogozen (District of Vratsa); height 4 cm, diameter 18.5 cm, weight 280.7 g. Last quarter of the 5th century BC? One of the most exquisite phials of the type 'dish' has been made in a typical for Persian craftsmen style. On its bottom (in the centre) an omphalos stands out, shouldered by a rosette composed by flower petals and framed by a wound wire. The frieze of figurines consists of four pairs of heraldic lions-griffons (with their heads turned backwards) separated by palmettos. The griffons have lion heads adorned with a horn bended powerfully backwards. They have spread their wings while their lengthen tails encircle leaf-like motif with palmettos.

**Phial from the Odryses Kings'
dinner set**
Silver with gilt. Treasure, the village
Rogozen (District of Vratsa); height 4
cm, diameter 17.5 cm, weight 177.8 g
Before 339 BC.
One of the two almost identical phials
of the type 'dish' on the bottoms of

which a raised girdle of bull heads
alternating with acorns is depicted.
The heads of the bulls are shown in a
'bird's view', by chiseling the master-
toreut has rendered the minute details
around the animal muzzle and horns.
On the frontlets of bulls there are
round decoration.

**Phial from the Odryses Kings'
dinner set**
Silver with gilt. Treasure, Rogozen
(District of Vratsa); height 2 cm,
diameter 13.6 cm, weight 184 g.
Before 339BC.
The essence of the mythological
scene presented on this phial can be
perceived from the inscription AYГE
ΔHΛAΔH , meaning "Auge (is) real".
Also in Greek another inscription
reads Didykaimo, meaning "Didy's
value" or "Assigned value of Didy"
(coming from the name Didy and
'kaymo' from the Balkan 'kayme',

'kaymet' from 'qawata' which means
'assign price/value/tax, appraise, rise'.
The Princess of Tegea, Auge, daughter
of the Arcadian King Aleos, being the
priestess of Athena of the name Aleos
is shown almost undressed, recoiling
from the one who tries to rape her. This
man, who is obviously somewhat tipsy,
is naked and with a wreath on his
brow. He holds Auge who pulls aside
with his right arm, across the thigh of
his right leg is seen the lion skin he has
pulled down from himself, and to the
left he has thrown his shepherd's crook
and quiver.

THE TREASURE OF BOROVO

This treasure was also found by accident. It was brought to light in 1974 when found during deep ploughing of one of the cultivated fields of the town Borovo. It consists of 5 silver vessels: a cup, rhyton-like pitcher, three rhytons with protomes of a horse, a bull and a winged sphinx. It has been assumed that this is only a part of the treasure as it was buried in 'two parts'. In any case, however, these vessels are part of Odryses' treasury plundered by Phillip II the Macedon, i.e. the finding from Borovo had also fallen in the hands of Triballs after they defeated Phillip II the Macedon in 339 BC.

This is easily made out from the identical Greek inscriptions on two of the rhytons and the rhyton-like pitcher. Translated they sound like 'To Kotys from Beo', and Kotys could be only the Odryses' King Kotys I (around 383 – 360 BC), while Beo occurs also on other vessels, found in the lands to the north of Stara Planina Range. The new owner of the treasury, some time after its sharing in 339 BC buried his share and this is suggested by the fact that no traces of long use show on the vessels.

On the mouth of the rhyton with horse protome a kind of 'monogram' of two letters, ΑΔ, is inscribed. K. Boshnakov has deciphered it as Αδαμας, an Odryses' aristocrat of 'King Medok's family', who was castrated by Kotys I in his childhood (the translation of the verb from Greek as "castration" is not very certain, it is quite possible that its meaning is "circumcision"). A similar inscription, three pointed hasts of Α or Δ can be seen on the bottom of the rhyton-like pitcher. The same 'monograms' have been hammered out also on the umbo and the mouths of two phials found near the village Alexandrovo and this was the reason to assume they formed, together with the treasure of Borovo, a special 'dinner set of Adamas'. The inscriptions 'To Kotys from Beo' seem to have been additionally hammered out after the Odryses' King had plundered 'Adamas' dinner set' because the latter had recanted from him.

However, it seems far more probable that the 'monograms' are a kind of abbreviation, version or unclear sacred formula of the kind ΔΑΔΑΛΕΜΕ, which occurs on Odryses Kings' vessels. It is not impossible in this case that the matter at hand is again some form of abbreviation of the name 'Adamas', not of the Odryses' aristocrat but of the 'Odryses' nymph' Adama (Ἀδάμας Ὀδρύσης Νύμφαις) known to us from a Dionysos relief from Paros from the 4th century BC (IG 12, 5, 245) and why not even from that 'Adam' by which the 'Orphic oath' was taken.

The most interesting piece of the treasure is the rhyton-like little pitcher with one opening. The rhytonizing of amphorae and pitchers in Europe seems to have been a Thracian patent and the inscription proves in an indisputable way that the little pitcher and the impressive scenes on it (also with certainty on the two rhytons at least) were made in a workshop in the privileged Thracian commune of Beo. The vessel is decorated with three friezes with figurines. It has been accepted that the upper frieze presents a Bacchanalian procession of 9 figures: of dancing maenads, satyrs, a silen and a male and female fig-

ures. On the lower frieze with figures three swans turned to the left are depicted. The central frieze is thought to have illustrated scenes from the 'Kabirs' mysteries'.

Here again, however, only the figures of the Boreads with wings spread 'down to their heels' can be seen with a relative certainty. Anatolian-Carian-Phoenician parallels of the Cabirs that guard the sailors, participation of Zetes and Kallais in the campaign of Argonauts, the 'Dragon' (a similar one, according to some versions, was erected on the bow of the ship 'Argo') and a number of other data have indeed raised the question of the existence of some ancient myth that has originated and developed in the environment of the Balkans, too that should yet to be investigated.

As a whole, the scene definitely illustrates 'Deities at feast' and the rhyton one of the gods holds in his hands is the most impressive piece. On it there is a griffon protome and the griffon head has a dentate crest. The griffon on the cup from this treasure is similar to the above and its more perfect (developed) version is known to us from the treasure of Letnitsa.

Rhyton with bull's protome

Silver with gilt. Part of the dinner set of King Kotys I (around 383 BC – 360 BC), manufactured in the Thracian settlement of Beo; treasure, the village Borovo (District of Rousse); height 16.5 cm, diameter of the mouth 9 cm. The rhyton is covered by horizontal flutes. The stylized forms, the decoration of the shorter horn, the overall structure of the vessel and, most of all, the posture of the bull betrays the Ahemenids' royal art influence. The head of the bull is somewhat stern and the legs (between which is the opening for the liquid) are bended. Similar vessels appeared also in Scythia where they have been dated from the first half of the 4th century BC. Rogozen findings, however, prove in an explicit way that vessels like this one were not an 'Ahemenid import' but locally made, in Odryses' royal workshops. This observation has far reaching consequences both for the postulated 'Scythian animal style' and for the nature and the ways of Iranian traditions penetrating Scythian lands as formulated by prof. M. Rostovtsev.

Rhyton with a horse protome
Silver with gilt. Part of the dinner
set of King Kotys I (around 383 BC
– 360 BC), manufactured in Thracian settlement of Beo; treasure, the
village Borovo (District of Rousse);
height 20.2 cm, diameter of the mouth
10.46 cm.
This rhyton is of the long-horn type
and ends with the protome of a one-
horned horse presented quite realistically. Between its legs the opening for
liquids is installed. The mouth is decorated with pearls while the neck is cov-

ered with a frieze of ivy twigs. They
meet at the front of the vessel where
bunches of fruits frame a birdie. The
separately cast elegant gold frieze is
soldered additionally to the neck of the
rhyton. The vertical part of the vessel is covered in flutes and is soldered
to the protome. To whom this rhyton belonged is something indubita-
ble because of the inscription on it:
ΚΟΤΥΟΣ ΕΞ ΒΕΟ, i.e. "To Kotys
from Beo" inscribed in dotted lines
(technique called poinçon) on the bottom of the vessel.

Rhyton with Sphinx protome
Silver with gilt. Part of the dinner
set of King Kotys I (around 383 BC
– 360 BC), manufactured in Thracian
settlement of Beo; treasure, the village
Borovo (District of Rousse); height
16.5 cm, diameter of the mouth 9 cm.
This rhyton ends with separately
affixed protome of exquisitely made
winged sphinx: head of a woman with
a body of a lion. The face is crowned
by the hair put up in a bun and tied
round by two ribbons. Punched ears
mark the missing ear-rings, while
the neck is embraced by a necklace

made of beads and leaf-like pendants.
The breast part of the sphinx, in a
Persian manner, is covered with
feathers (they are carefully hammered
out and the wings are additionally
soldered) and the rhyton could be
easily identified as a production of an
Ahemenid's workshop if there wasn't
an inscription. It is, however, beyond
doubt that this rhyton was made in an
Odryses' royal workshop because of
the inscription ΚΟΤΥΟΣ Ε[Ξ] ΒΕΟ,
i.e. 'To Kotys from Beo', engraved by
dotted lines (poinçon) on the mouth of
the vessel.

Odryses' royal dish: a cup for 'snow water'

Silver with gilt. Part of the dinner set of King Kotys I (around 383 BC – 360 BC), manufactured in Thracian settlement of Beo, treasure, village Borovo (District of Rousse); height 36 cm, max. diameter 29 cm.

This cup has two knee-joint handles and a stem decorated along its edge with ovoid ornament. The handles slid into openings located on the upper end of applications presenting impressive gulded heads of satyrs. On the bottom a Thracian scene is depicted: eagle-like griffon prepares to jab its beak into a lying roe-deer. This type of cups are considered as 'flat dishes', but it is possible to have served as containers for collecting 'snow water'. Such vessels were also in use in Thrace as we have learned from the work of Atheneos "Learned table-companions" (Dipnosoph., 4, 131a) in which a feast offered by King Kotys I when he marries his daughter to Iphicrates is described: "…Iphicrates was given as a portion two herds of white horses, a herd of goats, a gold shield, a flat cup (phial) for drinking wine, a helix-like, a bowl, a vessel for snow water, an earthen jag with millet, a 12-cubit long underground storeroom full of onion and a multiped hecatomb [25 heads of cattle]."

'Snow' in Thrace was collected in winter and it was kept in special storehouses. The 'snow water' was valued very much in summer when Thracian elite drunk it with pleasure in time of hot weather. Mostly, however, the snow water was used to dilute (and cool down) wine. Storing snow in special storerooms adjacent to wells and in deep cellars was widely practised in Thrace until the time of the modern refrigerators.

Rhyton-like little pitcher

Silver with gilt. Part of the dinner set of King Kotys I (around 383 BC – 360 BC), manufactured in Thracian settlement of Beo;, treasure, the village Borovo (District of Rousse); height 16.5 cm, diameter of the mouth 9 cm. This pitcher is covered with three friezes with figurines, which are interpreted as related to the mystery rites of the cult of Kabirs. The first frieze is a Bacchanalian procession. In the centre of the second one are depicted a woman and a man sitting, turned to the left. The man is bearded, has an ivy wreath on his brow and holds in his hands a rhyton with a sphinx protome and a phial, right opposite to the woman with the ribbon. On the right side there is a satyr who rests his right-hand elbow on a pitcher, and one can see a rhyton with protome of a crested griffon and phial (like the one for holding 'snow water') in his hands. The only more or less certain figurines are those of the Boreads, Zetes and Kalais, 'with wings reaching down to their heels', and depicted with radiant crowns on their heads. As a whole the story in pictures seems to illustrate a scene of the kind 'Feast of Gods'. On the third frieze are depicted birds catching fish. This suggests the need of abundant water and additionally points out to the possibility the scene from the central frieze to be thought of as the 'Feast of Gods' and to relate it to Thracian spring-summer rites of public prayers for rain. The big vessel placed under the lion head with wide opened jaws also makes one to assume this might be the case.

THE TREASURE OF LOUKOVIT

This treasure was an accidental finding made in 1953 followed by two more findings, in 1955 and in 1986. In all, the treasure consists of 15 silver vessels, 23 applications and requisites for horse harness, along with more than 200 silver rings, hemispherical buttons, and tubules, little applications of human and animal little heads. Three iron reins with bronze teeth suggest the treasure contains parts of three sets of decorations for horse harness. Unfortunately, part of these sets has been hidden (or lost) after the treasure was first found in 1953.

What impresses with some of the objects from this treasure is the sign of 'X', formed by two triangles meeting at their apexes. In Lycian alphabet for instance 'X' was pronounced 'ah' but it is possible in this case the sign to have had some ritual-magic symbolism. This observation was additionally supported by the fact that such a sign is put on Bulgarian ritual breads and is called 'Krastashka' (derivative from 'cross'), without giving it the meaning of the symbol of Christ at all. This 'Krastashka' can be seen in Bulgarian runic letters, too as well as in the calendar 'tallies'. The figure of 'eight' in various shapes can also be seen on Bulgarian ritual breads and some more enthusiastic researchers even see the stylized symbol of power, the hatchet. The sign on this phial also represents a 'labrys' which is interpreted as the symbol of the Odryses' dynasty because it is found on royal coins minted from the time King Medok reigned on (after 405 BC). The images of the Great Thracian Goddess in both her main hypostases have allowed researchers to accept that in this particular case the 'labrys-Krastashka' has some bearing to the rites related to annual change of seasons (or the nundial years) and the cults of the 'Mother-Earth' and her daughter, the Goddess-Virgin. It is indicative that in the 'Iberian alphabet' the same sign stands for the letter 'M', while a 'labrys' of the type of 'Krastashka' has been incised on the neck of another high phial from the treasure. If we accept for the 'labrys-Krastashka' the meaning of the letter 'M' then it might be (even though hypothetically) to assume it is an abbreviation of the name of King Medokos or of the Goddess-Mother (from 'Ma' or 'Me').

Phial
Silver with gilt. Treasure, town of
Loukovit, height 7 cm.
Second quarter of the 4th century
The phial from Loukovit is of the
'Ahemenid' type, with a hemi-spherical
body, relatively big smooth neck and
strongly protruding mouth edge. The
body below the neck of this high phial
is covered with female heads in full
face, separated by palmettos. The heads
are eight, their features are gracefully
rendered but their appearance is stern.
Below them, along the arc towards the
bottom of the vessel there is a second
frieze of eight female heads. The female
heads most likely symbolize the Great
Thracian Goddess (the upper frieze)
and the Goddess-Virgin (the lower
frieze). This repeating number of eight
according to some of the analyses
might be related to a 'mystery rite
of the 8-year way of immortalization
of Thracians'. If such a 'calendar'
approach to these images is allowable
at all in this case, then it is rather
more likely to look for an echo from the
ancient nundial calendar where the
week has eight days.

Loukovit treasure
Silver with gilt. Treasure, town of Loukovit; 15 silver vessels (6 higher phials, 5 lower phials and 4 pitchers), 23 applications of at least three suites for horse harness each, more than 200 silver rings, hemi-spherical buttons, tubules, little applications with images of Orphic and animal heads.
Third quarter of the the 4th century BC.

The mixed nature of this treasure is suggested both by the three sets of horse harness and by the silver vessels. The type, shape and decoration of the 15 vessels show that they undoubtedly have been a part of the Odryses' royal dinner sets, work not of Triballs but of workshop in South-East Thrace that have remained anonymous. Little human heads symbolizing Orpheos deserve special attention.

Applications for horse harness
Silver with gilt. Treasure, town of
Loukovit; max. diameter 8.3 cm.
Third quarter of the the 4th century BC
The two applications for vertical straps
from the treasure show galloping riders,
one turned to the right and the other,
to the left. The horsemen are with curly
hair and beardless and their chlamydes
wave behind them in the wind. The
decorated headstalls and breast-bands
of the horses are rendered in great
detail. The rider that is turned to the
right holds in his right hand a spear
pointed downwards where, under the
front hooves of the horse there is a fallen
lion. The lion has turned its growling
muzzle up towards the horseman and
can be told by his typical tail. The
horseman that is turned to the left
holds the reins in his left hand and
between the horses's legs a fleeing lion
also can be seen. Usually, this scene is
interpreted as 'Thracian aristocrat out
on a dynastic sport'. However, it seems
more likely to look for its place among
Thracian ritual cycles where the role
of the God-Horseman (along with the
Great Goddess) in the ritual killings
(and resurrections) in compliance with
the seasonal cycles within the year is
out of doubt.

Applications for horse harness
Silver with gilt. Treasure, town of
Loukovit.
Third quarter of the the 4th century
BC.
The two applications for horizontal
straps of the harness, in making of
which the technique of leaf gilding
has been used present the scene 'a lion
attacks a deer', in a motion to the left

and to the right, respectively. Deer are
fallow-deer, which can be told from
their antlers and the specific spots all
over their bodies. The stand of the deer
and the way the lion has bitten into it
allow making the conclusion that the
deer was not chased and caught but is
the so-called 'self-chased' deer, i.e. it
has offered itself as a sacrifice.

THE TREASURE OF LETNITSA

The treasure of Letnitsa has been found accidentally in 1963. It was covered by a bronze cauldron and at a distance of 7 or 8 m to one side of it a horse's rein was found. Under the cauldron there were 19 traditional by size and about 30 lesser applications for horse's harness along with scores of beads. The applications belong to two separate suites of decorations for horse harness that has not reached our time in their entirety.

Eight applications present the Thracian God-Horseman, clad in plated chain-mail and various scenes (in motion to the left or to the right). Their discovery proved the recognition won by the iconography of the Thracian God-Horseman (or Hero-Victor) which, by the middle of the 4th century BC, had already formed its basic subject-matters. Ivan Venedikov points to the typological connections between the Thracian horse deity and the 'Hittite Gods of Storm' but to him the Letnitsa treasure "presents for the first time the Thracian interpretation of a theogonic legend" in which part of the scenes present the intercourse between Demeter and Core with the God-Dragon, out of which liaison Dionysos-Zagreos was born.

The scenes on the applications pertain to at least three subject cycles. It seems that one group of applications presents the earliest European scenes of original 'duel of knights' between Gods/Heroes. Four applications reflect a Thracian plot which later, after having been deeply modified, would be laid in the foundation of the Bulgarian folklore fairy tales, too. The third group of applications was made by a more skilled craftsman and (with the exception of the rather bigger application 'Bear hunting') illustrates in a zoomorphic code. Among the applications of this set impresses the appearance of heraldically set griffons rising above eagles.

Attempts made by A. and K. Boshnakov are curious as they, in the spirit of "Thracian Orphism" ascribe to this treasure an Orphic-calendar nature for a period of "eight solar years" of the "Thracian calendar", the "mystery rite in the 8-year long way of immortalizing Thracians". In so far as we are not certain that all applications have reached us, this hypothesis remains within the range of artful analyses. The same holds true for the "fourteen ritual steps" and "the end of the five-year-period" when "entering of the young dynast into the circle of Thracian aristocrats-warriors" takes place. If such a hypothesis is yet acceptable to an extent when discussing some of the royal dinner sets because of the 'closed' character of their use, the appearance of 'covert' scenes on a ceremonial horse harness is absurd: then the craftsmen who made these applications should also have been "initiated in the mysteries" and this is unthinkable exactly in view of their explicitly postulated 'closed' 'aristocratic' nature prevailing in Thrace. Generally speaking, to 'reveal' in images the secret mysteries of 'immortalization' would have been to the ancient way of thinking a greater sacrilege than to have them relate or write down by sacral text formula. According to a version, Orpheos had been struck down by a lightning exactly because he dared to initiate Thracians in the mysteries, and even Herodotos (2.51) never gave a thought of mentioning anything specific related to Thracian mystery rites.

More of the scenes on the objects from Letnitsa treasure seem to really have the nature of a calendar and, very likely, is cyclical insofar as the Deities (both of the tillers of land and for the animal breeders) must be propitiated annually and following a fixed annual festal-ritual chronology in the course of permanent (saint) and 'movable' (astronomical) dates. At the same time the scenes from Letnitsa treasure have their good parallels not in Apulei character of Lucius from Book 11 of the "Golden Jackass", the Hittite beliefs, and the Nartian epos, but in Bulgarian folklore and traditional for Thrace seasonal rites.

The style analysis made by Iv. Venedikov shows that the applications were made during the reign of King Kotys I. Venedikov's observations and some other considerations allow placing the date of making the treasure in the second half of the 4th century BC: one of the suites in the time of Kotys I (around 383 - 360 BC) and the other (illustrating a zoomorphic code), in the time of his son King Kersebleptes (360-340 BC).

Applications of the type 'duel of knights'
Silver with gilt. Treasure, the village Letnitsa (District of Lovech); 7 of a total of eight (?) applications, grouped in pairs, in motion to the left (on the average about 5-cm high) and moving to the right (on the average about 4.5-cm high) with the exception of a single (its pair is missing) application, which is 4.5-cm high.
Third quarter of the the 4th century BC.
The applications with armed horsemen for a headstall of a horse harness form in a natural way opposite pairs. Those where the horseman moves to the right were on the left horizontal strap

of the headstall. They are a bit bigger (on the average by about 0.5 cm) and one of these is missing. Most likely it was an equal or mirror image of that from the right horizontal strap (the only bigger size right-side application, 5.4 cm high). There, the Hero with his hair arranged in battle hair-style of 'koukourigou' (literally 'cock-a-

doodle-doo' meaning a rooster's crest, with the hair tied on the head-top - this style is connected with the term 'akrokomoi') and a shield the type of 'pelta' slung on his back, sets off for his first feat. In all the three left-side applications the horseman, who rides on a stallion with its sex organ in erection and in the right-side move

has a companion, a 'cut-off head'. In
two of the applications the Hero has
long hair and beard, is clad in chain-
mail which covers his legs with the
feet, but in the third he is beardless.
Again in two of the applications he
carries his spear in his right hand
and in the third he has transferred

it into his left (the magical) hand.
The head is not cut off (as is usually
thought) but symbolizes 'Orpheos' who
'accompanies' the Hero as an 'advisor'
(in the Hittite texts these advisors are
always two, one for the left side of the
horseman, the other for his right side).
In two of the applications 'Orpheos'

looks down, towards the ground. In the third, exactly in which the Hero holds the spear in his left (the magical) hand and is already spruce and shaved (as Nartian also do) the other 'head-advisor' also appears (this time with new, changed hairstyle: its hair fall free down his shoulders) this time turned to the right towards the rider as if counselling him on something (to terminate the equal duel and to accept the proposal for fraternization?). From the opposite side and moving to the left (from the right-hand applications of the headstall) another hero advances to him, his outfit identical to the first

Hero. Behind his back in two of the applications a 'horse head' is put (in one of these applications it is with its back turned to him, looking to the right). In the third application the horse head is already replaced by a dog/wolf. 'The second advisor' has rested his legs in the horseman back as if whispering something into Hero's ear. As a result, the horseman has lowered his spear and a goblet has appeared in his left hand.

In the works so far published it has been accepted, this way or other, that these applications present scenes from Thracian royal or dynastic

acts (initiation of the Prince-Heir or admitting young dynasts into the circle of aristocrats-warriors). Respective parallels with the mythical Indo-Iranian precedents of the rite called 'Purushamedha' (human sacrifice) and 'Ashvamedha' (horse sacrifice) have been made. The striving to relate by all means these scenes with 'Thracian Orphic royal doctrine' about the 'King-Priest-God' has prevented researchers to perceive that, considered in their entirety (in view of the duels of the 'Gods of Storm' in the Hittite mythology and the data from the Nartian epos), they

in fact represent feats of the type of
'duels of knights' (after the model of
"They fought what they fought and
fraternized at the end of all"). This is
exactly what the outstretched forward
goblet (held in the left hand) depicts,
and the left hand here is exactly the
hand with which the fraternization
will be performed.

The application with the eight horse
protomes for the breast band of
the horse harness means that these
applications were intended to serve as
an original emblem of the whole set.

Application for horse harness
Silver with gilt. Treasure, the village
Letnitsa (District of Lovech); diameter
7 cm.
Second quarter of the 4th century BC.
The application is the breast-band
of that part of the harness that holds
the saddle in place and serves as an
original 'emblem' of the earlier suite
from the treasure. It is framed by an
edge of notches and below it there are

eight horse heads positioned in a raised
circle. The horse heads were engraved
together with the headstalls, leads and
distinctly marked manes. Part of horse
muzzles, the leads, the headstalls and
halters as well as the horses' manes are
gilded. The number of the horse heads
might be a resonance of the number
of the days in a week of the nundial
calendar. On the backside it has a ring
to hold the leather strap.

Application for horse harness

Silver with gilt. Treasure, the village Letnitsa (District of Lovech); height 6.5 cm.

Second quarter of the 4th century BC. A scene from Thracian mythology is presented on this application: a Nereis riding in Amazonian manner, a Dragon with horse head and a dentate crest (type Hippocampos, or sea horse). The sex of the figure is marked by two dots where her breasts are. Ivan Venedikov analyses the scene as a part of the 'Thracian legend of the theogonic legend' in whose Hellenic version Zeus appeared before Demeter or Core as a Dragon: with "her left hand the Goddess caresses a big dragon and with her right hand, his body". That's why it was possible in this particular case to have 'preparation' for the well-known also in Bulgarian folklore scene of the 'wedding of the dragon'. The position and gesticulation of woman's arms, however, rather exclude the 'caressing'. The 'Nereid' most likely stands for that Goddess (and/or Princess), which the Thracian Hero rescues from the Three-headed Dragon/Lamia.

Application for horse harness
Silver with gilt. Treasure, the village
Letnitsa (District of Lovech); height
6.5 cm.
Second quarter of the 4th century BC.
On this application a scene from
Thracian mythology is shown: a
human figure with the hair tidied up
on top of the head stands upright to the
left of a three-headed Dragon. On the
dress there is no indication for the sex
of the figure as in previous application,
therefore it could be assumed it is
a male figure. In his right hand he
carries a 'Mirror' of the kind the God
Hephest used to make: with the help
of such a mirror the watcher was able
to 'catch' every living thing. It is
levelled at the Three-headed Dragon/
Lamia because to catch with a 'mirror'
a creature from the World Beyond
was, to the archaic mythological
consciousness, equivalent to render
it harmless. According to some
analogies, this was the 'Golden Apple',
while Ivan Venedikov sees portrayed
a Goddess who again 'caresses' the
Dragon. The scene has good parallels
also in the Nartian epos as well as
in Bulgarian folklore (both in fairy
tales and in ritual practices). Another
parallel can be found in the famous
application from Hasandu from the
beginning of the first millennium BC.

Application for horse harness
Silver with gilt. Treasure, the village Letnitsa (District of Lovech); height 6.2 cm.
Second quarter of the 4th century BC. The scene on this application 'closes' the series of feats of the Hero. He himself is turned to the left and his long hair is tidied up on the top of his head, tied in 'koukourigou' (literrally 'cock-a-doodle-doo', but meaning 'the crest of a rooster'). The Hero possesses a woman who sits in his lap and has her face turned to him, hugging him tenderly. Behind her back another woman has fixed her gaze on the scene. According to Ivan Venedikov, this scene represents the sacred marriage of Core with Zeus who had changed his Dragon-like countenance with anthropomorphic one. The marriage was taking place "in the presence of Demeter (the Mother of gods) who holds the two material attributes: the vessel containing the sacred drink and the twig with which she gives her blessing to the divine couple". Out of their sacred marriage Zagreos would be born. Indeed, the Hittite parallels of the scene do not leave any trace of doubt that the woman with the 'twig' corresponds to the Goddess-Mother who gives a blessing to the Hero's marriage. With respect to who exactly are getting 'married' and who will be born as a consequence of the 'marriage' is not at all clear. Why not, for instance assume that this is Zeus' father, the Thracian 'Cronos' to whom the nymph

Trake will give birth to the first known to us European King, Dolonk (Δόλογκος), as is in the version told us by Arian in 'Bitynica'? Or maybe here the case in point refers to another Odryses' nymph, Adama, of whom we are aware from an ancient-Greek inscription dated from the 4th century BC?
The twig the Goddess holds in her left hand has a special interest. This twig 'hangs' over the two images and possibly illustrates a 'sourvakar' rite of the New Year blessing. The rite of 'sourvakane' (tapping people on the backs with a fresh, budding cornel twig wishing them a happy new year). The meaning of this rite performed with a freshly cut cornel twig is to transfer the life-giving strength of the cornel-tree to those blessed (people, houses, farm animals, fruit-trees, etc.) is typical for the Bulgarian New Year's cycle. This 'sourvakane' is a tradition performed by other peoples too, but as a rule during the autumn rites. Only in Bulgarians it is related to the New Year's blessings, while the "sourovachka" (the decorated cornel twig with little branches bended in a specific way) is a tool that was used in various – healing, mantic and other ritual practices. The observation that this scene might have an ancient-Thracian character is allowable because 'Thracian Hermes' also carries a big branch (cornel 'sourvachka') in a series of coins dated 386-375 BC of the Greek commune-little state in Thrace, Abdera.

Application for horse harness
Silver with gilt. Treasure, the village
Letnitsa (District of Lovech); height
5 cm.
Around the middle of the 4th century
BC.
Two notionally connected applications
present typical Thracian subjects. In
one of them a dog/wolf attacks a doe
running to the left, while the beast
has set its four feet on the doe back.
It has bitten its teeth into the doe
neck and its tail is raised in 'fighting
posture'. In the other application there
is a griffon 'attacking a deer'. The
griffon stands on the deer back, has
driven its beak into the neck of the deer
and the deer proper is a fallow one,
moving to the left and is lying down
onto the ground. On the backside of

these applications rings are affixed
to hold the straps threaded through
them. These applications are regarded
as an example of zoomorphic coding
of 'Thracian royal hunt' or 'a test of
values'. 'The Hero' is personified in
this case by the griffon while the dog
in Thracian scenes accompanied him
while he performed his feats. Bulgarian
rites related to the 'self-chased deer'
that came all by itself to the altar,
to be sacrificed allows for another
deciphering of the 'zoomorphic' code.
At the same time, in Bulgarian folklore
from Eastern Bulgaria there is a song
about a shepherd who failed to prepare
enough fodder for the winter and
his herd died out in the period from
'Christmas ('Koleda' in Bulgarian
tradition) through March'. Without

skinning the dead animals the shepherd piled the bodies up, placed on the top of this pile the "ram-'yugich'" and climbed up and stood himself on its top playing the kaval (shepherd's flute). Along with the version influenced by the Bible (after the herd died out completely the shepherd was not able to offer sacrifice to god on the day of St. Georges and following God's suggestion he slew his child in order to revive both his herd and the child). In Eastern Stara Planina Range there was a song about this 'means', while the solution was offered by St. Georges: in order to put an end to the fatal illness the herd 'had to be given to suckle the milk of a doe'. Here we see an animal-breeder's interpretation of ancient notions known to us from

the information passed down the ages by Hesiodes: "…when in the East the Atlantids [the Pleiads, the seven sisters of Atlantis] start to rise in the mornings, you have to hurry to reap the fields and when they begin to set down in the West, to sow!" Having in mind that the heliastic rise of the constellation of Pleiades in 8th-7th centuries BC at Thracian latitude began around 10th of May and its setting, by the beginning of November, we can compute the chronology of the basic cycle in Thracian animal-breeding and land-cultivating rites. The belief in the healing power of the doe milk allows for perceiving in these applications, too the cult notions related to the annual seasonal Thracian rites.

Application for horse harness

Silver with gilt. Treasure, the village Letnitsa (District of Lovech); height 8.6 cm.

Around the middle of the 4th century BC.

Here we have the picture of a horseman riding on a stallion. He has long hair and beard, clad in chain-mail, trousers and greave decorated with human head known to us from the 'Knee-piece from Adzhigoyl'. Similar knee-piece but with the image of the Great Thracian Goddess has also been found in the Mogilanska Mogila (the barrow Mogilan, town of Vratsa). Under the hooves of the horse there is a wolf/dog, while the point of his spear is trained on the head of a bear. On the back of the Hero three sticks arranged

in a plain are seen, which (because of the parallel with the cold comb from Soloha) depict a shield. According to what we know about Thracian notions the bear is related to Thracian Artemis but the Gettan Basileus Zalmoks was told to have been born on (or diapered in) bearskin. The scene has its ancient-Hittite parallels: in a Hittite inscription from 17th century BC about the war with 'Halpa': the enemy is described as a bear caught in its den, and the King-Hero is compared to a lion. In Bulgarian folklore on the other hand the most intelligent dweller of the Bulgarian forests, the bear (the 'tamest' among the 'wild beasts') is the main enemy of wolves and this perhaps turns it into the likely killer of the wolf/dog.

Application for horse harness
Silver with gilt. Treasure, the village
Letnitsa (District of Lovech); height
4.7 cm.
Around the middle of the 4th century BC.
The application presents 'wrestling'
bears: in Thrace they ranked among
the sacred animals of that hypostasis
of the Great Thracian Goddess, which
corresponds to the Hellenic Artemis.
Alexander Fol excludes the bear from
'Thracian Orphism' but it occupies
an important position as early as in
Hittite beliefs and rituality: in 18th
century BC King Anitta brought to
a temple he erected in the conquered
city of Nesa "... a hundred and twenty
bears and various other beasts..." One

of the bears is with its 'tail between its
legs' and yields itself giving way to
the other. It is possible that this scene
symbolizes the change of the basic
cycles in Thracian seasonal calendar.
In Bulgarian folklore the notion also
exists of the step-mother who had sent
her stepdaughter to 'wash black wool
until it is turns white at the end'. The
'Old lady' happened to pass by; she
liked the hard-working young girl and
turned the wool 'golden'. The step-
mother hurriedly sent her own lazy
and foul-mouthed daughter, which the
'Old lady' turned into 'Bear'. Perhaps
it was because of this metamorphosis
that the bears of the Balkans frequently
fell in love with Heros.

Application for horse harness
Silver with gilt. Treasure, the village
Letnitsa (District of Lovech); height
3.4 cm.
Around the middle of the 4th century
BC.
These applications are four (out of a
total of 8 applications from the set, 3
of which are broken to pieces and 1
has not reached the museum's stock).
There are pairs of griffons depicted,
positioned in a heraldic order with
their heads turned backwards, standing
above two oppositely situated eagles
and having set a foot each on palmetto.
Here, the higher craftsmanship in
making these applications suggests

that they were made by the same
toreut who had created the applications
with the fighting lion, griffon and
serpents. This fact allows for ranking
them among the second (late) suite
of the treasure, which relates in a
'zoomorphic' code. Because of the
parallels with the griffons from a
Phoenician sarcophagus from Sidon
(410 BC) and some other observations
on the development of Thracian
toreutics, it will not be an exaggeration
to assume that these applications, too,
certify for the advent of an original
'Phoenician wave' in Odryses'
workshops in the 4th century BC.

Application for horse harness
*Silver with gilt. Treasure, the village
Letnitsa (District of Lovech); height
12 cm.*
*Around the middle of the 4ᵗʰ
century BC.*
*Two rich of gilt, open-work
applications present a swastika of the
type three-arm spiral. Around the
umbo three stylized heads of griffons
or of birds with great eyes and heavily*
*hooked closed beaks are positioned.
They belong to the later suite from
the treasure and have their sure
parallels in the applications from the
Mogilanska Mogila and the treasure
of Loukovit. Such birds may also
be seen on a jug and a revert-conic
goblet (gobele) from Rogozen treasure:
their best parallels are revealed in the
"Nartian epos", where a monstrous
bird with an 'iron beak' is described.*

Application for horse harness

Silver with gilt. Treasure, the village Letnitsa (District of Lovech); height 5 cm.

Around the middle of the 4th century BC.

Here a lion fighting with a griffon are presented. The griffon has managed to bite into the lion neck and the lion in its turn had pressed the griffon down with his paws and rips open its belly with a fore leg. Two large serpents also take part in the fighting: their bodies are smooth, only their protomes are covered in scales. This 'fighting' represents the cyclic rejuvenation of nature and the seasonal Thracian rituality, something suggested by the serpents shedding their skins.

THE TREASURE FROM BOUKYOVTSI

Several accidental findings from the barrows near the village Boukyovtsi are kept in the National Museum of Archaeology. Among them are some impressive things: 2 silver phials (of diameter 13 cm and 17.7 cm respectively); little silver pitcher decorated with flutes (8.3-cm high), a silver ornament with gilt consisting of chains, fibulas, little human heads (capitulam), rosettes, etc. of total weight 642.92 g; a forehead piece shaped like a falcon (3.8-cm high); an application in the shape of two connect-

ed lotus blossoms (2.8-cm high); silver goblet (gobele) with gilt (12.2-cm high).

The fine gobele makes strong impression. Under its mouth there is a frieze of engraved and gilded lotus blossoms, alternating with palmettos. The body of the goblet is covered with horizontal flutes and near its bottom there is a gold undecorated girdle. On the other hand, the forehead-piece presents one of the earliest stylized images of a falcon. The little pitcher has given the name 'type Boukyovtsi' to a number of fluted little vessels, the most numerous (19)

among them being those from the Rogozen treasure. The vessels from this treasure were dated from the very end of the 5th century BC till 339 BC. They are the work of master-toreuts from Odryses' royal workshop that has remained nameless (no inscriptions found), which operated in the region of South-East Thrace. The vessels from the barrow necropolis near the village Boukyovtsi are part of a dinner set. The local elite Thracian family had received it most likely as part of the loot that was due to it after the defeat of the Phillip II's army in 339 BC.

MOGILANSKA MOGILA

This barrow was excavated in 1965 in the very centre of the town of Vratsa. From it comes one of the two, proved for certain, Thracian hearse from pre-Roman times. Three burial chambers have been revealed, which form the under-barrow funeral complex. The salvage manner in which the excavations were carried out and the lack of good photo-documentation renders analyses of the findings quite difficult.

The most interesting is grave No. 2 where two horses were laid together with the chariot and separately there is a skeleton of another horse, a silver-plated rein and silver applications. Close by, the bones of a man and a spear were found. At a distance of about 3.5 m away, in the western part of the chamber the skeleton of a 'young man' was laid with his face to the ground. Here, near the head a gold crown was found along with 47 gold applications, 2 gold ear-rings, four silver phials, little silver pitcher, rhytonized little amphora, silver knee-piece with gilt on it, 88 spear points, a sword, bronze helmet, 50 clay figurines and other findings. The mirror placed near the left hand is of special value. The buried man (about 145-cm to 150-cm tall) was young and because of the many splendid ornaments was, until recently, reckoned to have been the beloved wife of the other buried (and even as an 'Amazon'). In fact ornaments in ancient Thrace had not been exclusively women's attributes and most likely in this case we have a buried Triball prince. An indication to this is the gold crown (of 24-cm diameter and weighing 205 g) and the fact that, along with the chariot, a horse was sacrificed, the silver applications for its harness being exceptionally rich (about 200 ornaments). It might be that the prince perished (together with the other Thracian, the chariot-driver?) during Alexander the Great campaign against the Triball King Syrmos in 335 BC.

The rest of the stock consists of vessels for wine and water, a candelabra and lamps, accoutrements (the famous knee-piece included), a mirror and other things. In the horse trappings there are combined round applications with little human heads symbolizing Orpheos, also observed in Loukovit treasure.

Rhytonized little amphora
Silver. Mogilanska Mogila, town of
Vratsa; height 14 cm, max. diameter
6 cm.
Before 339 BC.
The rhytonized little amphora is most
likely a part of an Odryses Kings'
dinner set. Its body has the shape of
a cone. The cone is inseparable part
of the Dionysos' thyrsos, which is a
long sceptre wrapped in ivy or vine
leaves ending on top with a pine cone.
Why the body of the little amphora
was decorated in this manner can be
concluded from the Euripides drama

"Maenads', in which one of the
maenads 'grabbed the thyrsos and hit
the rock: a jet of crystal clear water
spurted from it; another one threw the
thyrsos on the ground and to her the
God sent a spring of wine. Those of the
presented that wanted to drink a white
drink raked up the earth with the tips
of their fingers and found streams of
milk; from the ivy leaves sweet honey
trickled down." On the cone scales
there are also stylized raised symbols
of the Sun and in the case with this
particular little amphora the pine cone
gave wine to the drinking.

Little pitcher

Gold. Mogilanska Mogila, town of Vrastsa; height 9 cm, weight 240 g. Third quarter of the 4th century BC. The little pitcher is of the type with low stem and is part of the stock found in two burials, one a horse sacrifice and another of a chariot with the horses. The mouth of the pitcher is covered with pearls and ovulae, under its neck there is a wreath of palmettos, while the open-work handle has the shape of a "Hercules' knot". The walls of the vessel are occupied by two opposite two-wheel chariots with hanging chassis separated by a big palmetto. Four one-horned horses are put to the chariots, their bellies arranged in a straight line. The horses' headstalls and breast-bands are decorated with round applications. In each of the chariots there is a standing coachman, and the chariots themselves are winged: one can see four feathers on the back side of each. These feathers are additional indication helping to tell who the coachman is: he is the god Apollo. On these images he is beardless and rather naïve as a style: his hair is shown as parallel notches, the eyes are in their full length and the head is rather disproportionate compared to the body, which is visible to its waist only.

Knee-piece
Silver with gilt. Mogilanska Mogila,
town of Vratsa; height 46 cm.
Third quarter of the 4th century BC.
The upper part of the knee-piece is
given the shape of a woman face
with almond-shaped eyes and a brow
covered with an ivy garland. The
hair is conveyed by spiral locks, on
the brow it forms a horizontal braid
and along both sides of the face long
ringlets shaped like serpent's bodies fall
freely down. On the neck they change
into lion figurines forming an original
torque. From the ears hang earrings
shaped like birds. The wide bands on
the face probably mark a tattoo. The
two serpents with lion heads (as seen
from above) coming out from snails'
shells, the heads of lion-griffons, on one
of which an eagle of huge talons has
set feet and from the other a wing is
coming out, suggest that they present
the image of the Great Goddess in her
hypostasis of Potnia terron.

Phial
Silver with gilt. Mogilanska Mogila,
town of Vratsa; height 4.5 cm,
diameter 10 cm, weight 117.16 g.
Before 339 BC.
The body of this phial is covered with
flutes, while its bottom is decorated
with an application made by using the
technique of leaf gilding; in the centre
of a framed frieze there is a medallion
with the head of the Great Goddess in
profile. The Goddess has a luxurious
hair-do of the type of a 'bun' and wears
the typical earrings and necklace.
This phial together with the rest of
the phials (those with inscriptions
included, too) and along with other
findings from the stock of those buried
in the Mogilanska Mogila are part of
an Odryses' royal dinner set.

THE RHYTON FROM ROZOVETS

This rhyton has a low horn and is shaped quite realistically like a roe-deer's head. The front side of it has been damaged and its back side is altogether missing. A big ivy garland girds its entire neck. The ears of the animal are separately made and are additionally soldered to the vessel. The eyes are shown in their entire length (though in a side view) and have been inlaid in glass.

The rhyton horn is covered with a raised Dionysos' scene: two satyrs are enthralled in the rhythm of an orgiastic dance, while a third one (moving to the left) carries on his shoulder a cy-lix-like crater. The faces of all three figures are flat-nosed and have pointed ears.

Rhyton with a roe-deer head
Silver with gilt. Stock from Yuzhnata (the Southern) Mogila, the village

Rozovets (District of Plovdiv); height 16.3 cm, weight 449.5 g. The beginning of the 4th century BC?

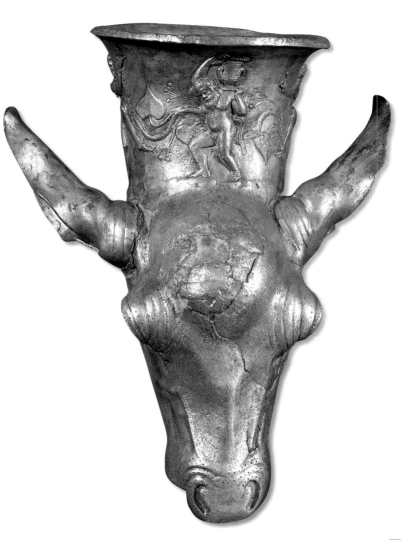

THE PANAGYURISHTE TREASURE

On December 8th, 1949, in the grounds of the ceramic factory Meroul, three brothers: Pavel, Petko and Michael Deykovs were digging clay for bricks. At a depth of about 2 m their shovels reached some yellowish objects. The brothers took them out of the clay, inspected them and came to the conclusion that all this is some 'hidden Gypsy brass instruments' and threw them carelessly aside. Residents of Panagyurishte crowded around to see the 'Gypsy brass music'; some even tried to blow the 'instruments' in order to become convinced in their practical uselessness.

Then, however, the then curator of the local museum, Dr. Petar Gorbanov, an alumnus of the University of Vienna, arrives on the spot. The disciple of the great archaeologist of the 19th century, Prof. F. Schachermayer does not accept the conclusions of the village 'experts' and organises the salvaging of the finding.

The treasure consists of nine vessels made of pure gold, of total weight 6165.45 g and is a part of a dinner set. According to Ivan Venedikov, the set had been completed in three times: first the three rhytons with animal heads were acquired, then the rhyton with goat's protome and the phial and finally the rhytonized amphora and the three rhytons shaped like female heads. He discusses the manner of making up the dinner set: the suite has not been full because another, fourth in a row, anthropomorphic rhyton was missing along with two more shaped like animals.

It seems more likely, however, that this dinner set is part of loot: its total value is 14 000 drachmas (in silver equivalent). The latest date of its being buried in earth is considered 280-279 BC when Celtic tribes had invaded Thrace.

Four of the vessels are rhytons, three are rhytonized pitchers, one is a rhytonized amphora (with two openings) and one is a big shallow phial. The three rhytonized pitchers were shaped like female heads, the three rhytons have the shape of animal heads, two of which are of fallow deer and one is like a ram's head. One of the vessels is a rhyton with a long horn and goat's protome.

Substantial contribution to understanding the finding was

made by Dr. Petar Gorbanov. He describes the amphora-rhyton as a vessel peculiar to Thrace and defined it as a 'rhytonized amphora'. According to him, such vessels were used during the rite of 'libatio'.

Maybe, in connection with the manner of using the rhytonized amphora, we will have to quote the following text by Herodotos about a Scythian tradition (4.66): *"Once a year, every leader of a region gave an order to make a mix of wine and water in a vessel. Every one of the Scythians who had killed enemies in battle was entitled to drink from this beverage. However, those who did not have such merits could not even touch the vessel: they sat aside, put to shame and to them this was the gravest disgrace. Regarding those who had happened to kill more enemies they drank from vessels with two openings* [variant: from two goblets combined in one]*."* During these ritual feasts warriors that had deserved fame in battles sat on the ground in a circle and passed to each other the full phials and goblets. This custom had also been testified to by Aristotle (Pol. 7.2.6) who wrote: *"With Scythians, during one of the holidays, they did not allow the warrior that had not yet killed even a single enemy to drink from the goblets passed around in a circle."* It seems likely that the large shallow gold phial was used exactly to that end: only those from the respective outfit that had distinguished themselves on the battlefield.

Two rhytons with a fallow deer also make an impression and they have some remote parallels in local beliefs in the self-chased deer. The legend and the cult of the self-chased deer that came on the fixed date and hour to the respective sanctuary and alone put its head under the oblatory knife has survived through millennia (The Gold Deer and the Gold Doe are extremely popular in the epos of North-Iranian peoples).

The origin of the treasure and the interpretations of the scenes on the vessels, however, still remain disputable. The origin of the treasure is likely to be related to the development of the relations between Lysimachos and Seuthes III after 323 BC.

At any rate, the entirely gold make of the Panagyurishte vessels shows an undoubtful 'Hellenistic' novelty to the local toreutics, no matter where and by whom they were ordered and manufactured.

Phial with Pygmies' heads

Gold. Treasure, town of Panagyurishte (District of Pazardzhik); height 3.5 cm, diameter 25 cm, weight 844.7 g. Before 280/279 BC.
Among the vessels from the treasure the gold phial is the best and most convenient vessel for drinking wine. The Pygmies' heads (a symbol of sexual potency) are depicted in negative form. They are supplemented by plant ornaments: nine-leaf palmettos, volutes, buds, etc. As a whole the phial falls in an odd disharmony with the rest of the vessels from the dinner set. Because of it as well as of some

other objects and scenes, the possible influences of the Phoenician toreutic school and the Carian-Phoenician earth-cultivating and communal cults on Thrace should be investigated from now on. These influences should perhaps be sought also in the sagas about the famous 'battle of the Pygmies with the cranes' that took place in Gerania, which is localised to the north of Odessos (today's Varna). 'The battle of Pygmies with the cranes' is depicted on some amphorae stamps from Sinope, and one such stamp is kept in Kavarna museum (not published yet).

Rhyton with goat's protome
Gold. Treasure, town of Panagyurishte
(District of Pazardzhik); height 14 cm,
weight 439.05 g.
Last quarter of the 4ᵗʰ century BC.
This rhyton is without handle and
ends with a goat's protome. From the
inscriptions in Ionian dialect (with
some attiques) it can be deduced that
a scene with Hera, Apollo, Artemis
and Nike is presented on it. In the
Greek mythology such a scene is unknown and that means that an unclear
Thracian subject is actually presented based on the Dionysos' rituality as
much as this god is known to have appeared under the guise of a goat, too.
The Goat features also in the proces-
sions of animals from some scenes on
the Rogozen treasure vessels and also
occurs on other Thracian objects. It
also has an essential meaning in Bulgarian 'koukers' rituality.

Rhytonized pitcher
Gold. Treasure, town of Panagyurishte
(District of Pazardzhik); height 21.5
cm, weight 466.75 g.
Last quarter of the 4th century BC.
The vessel has a smooth neck separated
from the spherical body by a pearl
and ovulae and its four-edge handle
ends at the top with a sphinx. On her
heck the 'woman' (with a sumptuous
hair-do divided into two parts), who
symbolizes the Great Goddess (in
her hypostasis of Bendida) wears a
necklace. In the middle of the necklace
there is a medallion with lion head and
the opening for drinking is set into
lion mouth. The wings of the lion are
cut off (it is not known when this has
happened: perhaps during the sharing
of the loot in the antiquity?). The other
rhyton of the pair is almost identical
to this one.

Rhytonized pitcher

Gold. Treasure, town of Panagyurishte (District of Pazardzhik); height 20.5 cm, weight 387.3 g.

Last quarter of the 4th century BC.

The pitcher was moulded like the head of an Amazon (according to some of the analyses like the head of Athena) the neck of which serves as the bottom of the vessel. On the smooth neck a necklace shows up with a medallion with a lion head in the middle. The drinking opening is set in the lion mouth and this determines the pitcher as a rhytonized one. The 'Amazon' to the Thracians from the early-Hellenistic epoch is on principle equivalent to Thracian Goddess-Virgin (= to Bendida). The face of the goddess is correctly outlined, her hair is lush and curly and falls down in straight tufts on the back side of the neck and from her forehead up the pitcher narrows and changes into a helmet of Thracian type (in the shape of a fur cap). A plant element on the helmet separates two heraldically positioned images of griffons, quite carefully treated. The four-edge fluted handle ends at its upper end with a shaped base where a winged sphinx has squatted.

Rhyton

Gold. Treasure, town of Panagyurishte (District of Pazardzhik); height 13cm, weight 689 g.

Last quarter of the 4th century BC.
This rhyton is the mate of the other one, with the scene "Paris adjudging" depicted on it. It is assumed that on the neck of the rhyton two heroic scenes are presented. On one of them Theseos stalks the Bull of Marathon that used to devastate Athens. The beast was taken to Athens where the Hero offered it as a sacrifice to Apollo of Delphi. What strikes here is that, compared to the Bull of Marathon the figure of Theseus is somewhat awkward..

It seems that the craftsman was more proficient at depicting animals than humans and this perhaps suggest that the craftsman or the workshop were not Hellenic. On the other scene, Hercules had caught in the lands of the Hyperboreans the Kerinean Roe of Artemis which had golden horns and copper cloven hooves. The scene when first looked at has very good parallels in the Nartian epos where the most honourable hunt is that for the 'golden doe/roe', the daughter of the Sun. It sounds strange, however, that the roe has the antlers of a fallow deer, with Hercules catching it on the left one.

Rhyton

Gold. Treasure, town of Panagyurishte
(District of Pazardzhik); height 12.5
cm, weight 505.5 g.
Last quarter of the 4th century BC.
It is moulded as the head of a young
ram, evident from the budding horns.
On its lower lip there is an opening,
while the handle is moulded as an image
of a lion. On the neck there is a scene:
Dionysos sits on a throne, in his right
hand is a thyrsos (sceptre) and there
is a female figure by him, to whom the
inscription 'Eriope' refers. Eriope has
half-turned to the left and has embraced
Dionysos with her right hand, while
her left hand holds tenderly the divine
hand lain on her shoulder. On both
sides there are dancing maenads: one
of them holds a thyrsos and the other,

a thyrsos and a kettle-drum with
which she accompanies the wild dance.
The two figures are with their backs
to each other, wear chitons belted on
their waists and their upraised faces
betray the exultation of the dance. The
Dionysos' nature of the scene is out of
doubt because of the dotted inscription
'Dionysos'. The name of Eriope, known
to us only from Homer's Iliad (mother
of Ajax of Aokrya) is rather odd to find
in a Bacchanalian scene. In this case it
is either a craftsman's mistake (some
writers think he was not a Hellene
but a 'Barbarian toreut' and this was
the reason to inscribe wrongly Eriope
instead of Ariadna, wife and priestess
of Dionysos in some of the myths about
Theseus) or he was some unknown
Thracian mythological plot.

Rhyton

Gold. Treasure, town of Panagyurishte (District of Pazardzhik); height 13.5 cm, weight 674.6 g.
Last quarter of the 4th century BC.
The rhyton is moulded like the protome of a fallow deer, made with exceptional craftsmanship. On the deer frontlet there is a rosette with the ornamental motif 'rotating solar disk'. The opening is set on the lower lip of the animal. There are four figurines depicted on the animal neck, one of them is upright, the other three, sitting. The inscriptions, written in dotted lines specify the scene characters: the male figure belongs to the Trojan Prince Paris-Alexander and the three female figures are the goddesses Here, Athena and Aphrodite. The scene illustrates "Paris' Adjudging" from the mythological cycle of the Trojan War, which was popular with Thracian aristocratic circles. The Trojan Prince sits between Athena and Here with his gaze fixed on Zeus' wife. He is clad in short chiton, tight trousers, wears pointed shoes and has a pointed fur cap on his head. In his left hand he holds a shepherd's crook and his right one shows up behind the back of Aphrodite. He had already decided which one of the three goddesses is the most beautiful one. That is why Athena looks somewhat unbelievingly, while the image of Here emanates displeasure and wrath. The standing upright Goddess of love Aphrodite wins and it shows on her face and the content smile on her lips.

Rhytonized amphora

Gold. Treasure, town of Panagyurishte (District of Pazardzhik); height 20.5 cm, weight 387.3 g.

Before 280/279 BC.

Rhytonized vessels, though having unquestionable Iranian prototypes, in Europe they can be accepted on principle as a Thracian patent. The rhytonised amphora with two openings for drinking has so far found its close parallel in Scythia from where a similar vessel is known but with three openings (also a silver amphora is known from Sinope). The vessel undoubtedly unites the functions of a rhyton and an amphora. It has been assumed that it was used during the rite of 'fraternization' but probably has also served for 'purifying' liquids. There is not a single sure interpretation of the scenes: the attempts to place them on Greek (The Seven against Thebe, Achilles, Hercules's sons)) mythological or Macedonian (scenes from the life of Alexander the Great) royal foundations are not at all convincing. The same holds true if one is looking for parallels in the cult of Kabirs. Most likely, the case in point is about Thracian funeral ritual scene in front of the door of a monumental tomb. P. Tsatsov, after pointing out to the typically Thracian motifs (including the theme of Thracian dance with swords) took heed of an 'Etruscan parallel': with the two images to the left of the door Thracian toreut presents liver fortune-telling, as an important part of the funeral sacrifice".

THE APPLICATIONS
FROM MRAMOR MOGILA

In 1903, quite accidentally in Mramor Mogila near the town of Panagyurishte some silver applications were come across, the origin and the function of which are disputable. On principle the suites are divided into two parts: one part had been used for decorating a shield, while the other part was for a horse harness; and according to some of the authors all of them had been phaleras (for a shield or armor). The suites were dated from 7th till 4th century BC.

A suite for decorating a shield
Silver. Mramor Mogila, town of Pan-
agyurishte.
7th century BC?
In the centre of the suite there was a large oblong application (height 32 cm), decorated with human and animal figurines, portrayed rather naively. On the upper end a scene is *presented, which is assumed to illustrate the 'fight of Hercules with the lion of Nemeos'. 'Hercules, however, moves to the left, is not engage in fighting and has turned his back to the lion of Nemeus. In the lower end there is another figure, equal in size with 'Hercules', which is thought to be a 'Syrene' but is actually the*

Great Goddess in a dragon-like shape (She-Serpent or She-Dragon). She has eagle's legs, her body is turned full face, while her head and tail are portrayed half-face. In her right hand she carries unclear object (objects?) of double-conic shape, assumed to be a harp or revert-conic chalice (gobele?). Above her soars a winged griffon with the body of an ungulate animal (boar? With its tail curled and its bristle up). Under Hercules a winged animal, which also seems an ungulate is depicted.

The scene indeed has a 'Hellenic' parallel. It can be found in the version on the origin of Scythians as told by Herodotos (4.8-10). It was exactly from the union of Hercules with a creature half-goddess/half-serpent inhabiting a cave that Agatyrs, Gelon and Skit were born, the eponyms of the Thracian tribes of Agatyrses (inhabiting for sure the lands of today's Banat), the Gelons and the Scythians, the latter living in a country 'now called Scythia' (ἐς τὴν νῦν Σκυθίην χώρην καλεομένην). Among the round applications from this suite (8 to 95.5 cm) what makes an impression is the one representing a pair of animals and a bird. In the spirit of structuralism the expert in arts Ivan Marazov describes it in the following manner: "Around the round umbo (the centre of the world) three animals are shown: an eagle (the upper zone of the Cosmos), a lion (the middle one) and a boar (the lower one)."

The scene, however, has definitely ritual characteristics because one of the animals (the lion) is belted, i.e. it is a sacrificial animal. The heads of the animals on the other hand are directed towards an altar (or a 'Tree of life') and their tails are separated by a bird (eagle?) that also has set its feet on a rock (altar?).

Applications from a "Suite for decorating horse harness"
Silver. Mramor Mogila, town of Panagyurishte.
5th century BC?
These applications are ten: two round and big (diameter 5.5 cm) representing 'Hercules in a fight with the lion of Nemeos' and on the remaining eight (of 5.5-cm diameter) a head with a crown of laurels is portrayed. The appearance of the

eight square plates does not allow to determine for sure what their function had been: applications for a horse harness (all of them have rings on their back side for the straps) or phaleras for a shield or armor. The head of Apollo portrayed on them wears a crown of laurels and on the crown, on the eyes and on the lips traces of gilt show up.
The rings for the straps contradict the fact that the plates have rather

roughly drilled openings along the edge (on one of them in the upper right corner there are even two openings). At first glance, this suggests their second-hand use: as phaleras for a shield or for armor. The fact that most of the plates have their ends missing suggests that the plates with Apollo's heads on them have also been used as votive offering. The practice to place bronze and silver images on the joints or to affix them as original votive offerings on the walls of built temples or rock sanctuaries was until recently related to the early Semitic cultures. A silver plate with images of 'Sabasius' from the wall of the Rodopa Mountains rock sanctuary Belintash points to the fact that a similar custom had existed in Thrace, too. Thus, among the functions of those plates of paramount importance is the votive offering one (donations to the God-Sun).

A SUITE FOR HORSE HARNESS FROM KRALEVO

In the vicinity of the village Kralevo (District of Targovishte) there is a Thracian necropolis consisting of seven barrows. In one of them, namely Mogila No. 3, in 1970 a burial was found in which the incineration of the corps was studied. The stock of the treasure consists of 47 objects among them being: a breast-plate, a wreath of bronze, clay and wooden elements with gilt, gold earrings with lion heads on them, two silver serpent-like bracelets, an axe, strigila and iron reins with 'zabalets' the type of 'echini' (hedgehog). Such reins appeared in the second half of the 4th century BC. Along with the rein goes a set of applications for the headstall and the leads: a nose-plate or frontlet-piece and six gold applications for horse harness framed in ovulae: two applications are square and present griffons with dentate crests, standing at opposite ends; four of the applications are of round shape and present the head of Thracian Hercules with a hood made of lion skin.

The suite is made entirely of gold, while the decoration is executed in the techniques filigree, granulation and enamel. The use of gold in this section of Thracian toreutics, along with the appearance for the first time of the filigree enamel in Thrace, also marks the penetration of some new trends in local jeweller's art in the second half of the 4th century BC.

Nose-plate or a frontlet-piece
Gold and glass paste. Mogila No. 3 from the necropolis near the village Kralevo (District of Targovishte); height 4.4 cm.
Second half of the 4th century BC. The nose-plate has the shape of the figure eight presented as a large palmetto from the middle of which a plastic eagle's head comes out, an eagle griffon. It could have been also a frontlet-piece which, because of its relatively small size, was not curbed in an arch-like way along the horse frontlet. The 'eight' is assumed to have been a strongly stylized image of one of the Thracian royal symbols: the labrys. The nose-plates from Brezovo, Orizovo, Teteven, Toros, Shipka, Starosel, etc, fall under this Thracian type as well the frontlet-pieces from Boukyovtsi, Mezek, findings from Bessarabia and the Ukrainian steppes.

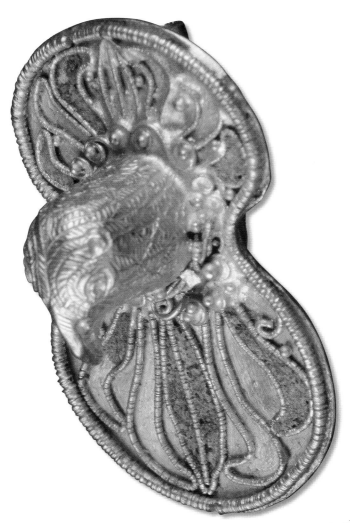

Applications for the horizontal strap of the halter
Gold and glass paste. Mogila No. 3 from the necropolis near the village Kralevo (District of Targovishte); height 3.6 cm. length 4.6 cm. Second half of the 4th century BC. The two rectangular applications have been set on the opposite ends of the horizontal bands. On them, two griffons are presented in relief. They have the bodies of winged lions and heads of eagles, in a motion to the left and right respectively. They undoubtedly have apotropeic functions. The same patronizing functions have the griffon, the Dragon (or the She-Dragon) and even the Lamia in Bulgarian folklore and ritual practices, which is the distinguishing trait of Bulgarian folk culture and points to its deep north-Iranian (Thracian) roots.

SILVER SUITE FROM RAVNOGOR

In 1987, in an under-barrow backfill of the Thracian necropolis near the village Ravnogor (District of Pazardzhik) the archaeologist Georges Kitov excavated silver applications for horse harness. The suite contains: a frontlet-piece, seven round applications and several scores of silver beads (of diameter around 1.2 cm, in some of them even the double cord has been preserved, on which they had been strung up). Six of the applications are grouped by pairs, which have performed the functions of side covers on the horse's head. The first pair (of diameter around 7 cm) is with Athena busts on them. The Goddess wears a helmet with a crest and a shield can be seen behind her shoulder, and in one of the images a spear shows up, too. On the second pair (of diameter about 7 cm) the busts of Nike emerge, whose wings are rendered in great detail. The third pair (of diameter about 6.5 cm) has as a decoration the busts of the Goddess-Virgin. The Thracian Goddess-Virgin can be told by the upper end of the quiver with arrows, which shows up over her right shoulder. The seventh application was for a breast-plate and presents the syncretic Hellenistic notions of Thracians about the Great Goddess.

Application for horse harness
*Silver with gilt. The village Ravnogor
(District of Pazardzhik); diameter 28 cm.
3rd century BC?
The application is bigger than the
other six but has reached our time
in damaged state. It served as a
decoration (and for linking together
at the same time) the harness on the
horse breast and presents an elegant
bust of a young woman, with beautiful
expressive face and naked tender neck.*

*From her shoulders wings come out, a
wreath shows up on her brow and her
hair ribbon falls down onto one of her
wings. The bust has a syncretic nature,
which is perceived also both because of
the ivy wreath and the animal shoulder
visible on the breasts. The image
perhaps syncretic functions of Athena,
Nike and Artemis and illustrates the
Hellenistic notions of Thracians about
the Great Goddess tallying with what
we know about Bendida.*

THE YAKIMOVO TREASURE

The treasure was accidentally found during excavation works in 1972 near the village Yakimovo, district of Montana. It contains 4 silver revert-conic cups, a silver кantharos, 2 round applications (with two of the cups), 2 massive silver bracelets, a bronze vessel, fragments from a bronze strainer (for filtrating wine) and bronze grip for a situla (bucket).

The attempts of K. Boshnakov and A. Boshnakova at interpreting the treasure as a 'Dinner set of the Triunity' where one of the cups was a 'Vessel for the God', the second one, a 'Vessel for the Goddess' and the third one, a 'Vessel for the mist' are not convincing. Anyway, the cups are four and not three, and the silver cantahros has been excluded from the 'Triunity'.

The treasure from Yakimovo is in fact one of the best examples of what the wine sets actually consists of, after the wine proper is 'purified' and possibly 'mixed' or 'diluted'. For the bronze strainer testifies explicitly on the process of purifying the wine, the wine being poured initially in the missing bronze bucket, an evidence of which is its grip.

On the presented silver revert-conic cup, which is the biggest one, a God-Horseman is portrayed moving to the right but unfortunately his image is much damaged.

The head of the horseman looks, as the Thracian manner is, full face. He is heavily armed and carries his sword in its scabbard, while the horse (moving to the right) seems, like its rider, to be protected by a chain-mail. Thus, the image presents one of the earliest known to us heavily armed warriors of the type 'knight'. Two silver applications had been additionally soldered to the bottoms of the cups. One of them shows a bust of the Great Goddess and the other, of the God-Horseman.

The cups have been expertly balanced because when full they stand upright but when empty, tilt to one side.

Silver revert-conic Thracian cup
Silver with gilt. Village Yakimovo
(District of Montana); height 10.5 cm,
max, diameter 17.2 cm
2nd – 1st centuries BC.

Revert-conic cup
Silver with gilt. Village Yakimovo
(District of Montana); height 8 cm,
max. diameter 15.2 cm.
2nd-1st centuries BC?
An application with a bust of a
bearded god in very deep relief has
been affixed on the bottom of the cup.
The image is with abundant gilt.
The torque around the neck makes
impression, while the manner of its
making contrasts with the bust of the
Goddess from the other cup.

Revert-conic cup
*Silver with gilt. Village Yakimovo
(District of Montana); height 10.2 cm,
max. diameter 16.5 cm.
2nd – 1st centuries BC*

*A bust of a goddess is affixed on the
bottom of the cup, in deep relief with
abundant gilt and with a torque on
the neck.*

Nose-piece from a horse harness
Silver with gilt. Village Sveshtari
(District of Shoumen); height 7.4 cm,
weight 43.65 g.
Last quarter of the 5th century BC?
The nose-piece (or plate) from
Sveshtari is of oval shape covered
with images and ornaments. In
the publications, this finding has
been defined as a frontlet-piece
but actually it is a nose-piece (or
plate) because of its flat base (the
frontlet-pieces are with oval base).
The central image presents three-
dimensional beardless head of a man,
whose hair is divided into tufts by
polygons. On both sides of the neck
there are holes, most probably where
the vertical strap passed. Under the
man's head a lion head is engraved,
'viewed from above'. Wings suggest
that the composition was able to fly
(a god or a hero mounted on a lion).
The nose-pieces and the frontlet-
pieces on principle functioned as
decorations (without any practical
importance) and they were affixed
on horizontal or inter-ocular vertical
straps. One can get a satisfactory
notion of them from the murals in
the tomb 'Mogila Tyulbe' (town of
Kazanlak), while the pictures in the
Alexandrovo tomb present together
both nose- and frontlet-pieces. The
only function one could ascribe to
the frontlet-pieces is to keep away the
tufts from the horse mane that fall on
its frontlet.

Scyphos
Silver with gilt. Mogila Orela II, town of Strelcha (District of Pazardzhik). 4th century BC.

The scyphos from Strelcha belongs to the so far rarely found in Thrace classic type of deep chalices with two, horizontally positioned handles. It is made of thick sheet of laminated silver and individual elements have been gilded using the technique of leaf gilding. Images have been stamped using relief stamps. Additional engraving was also used, which shows well in female heads. The decoration is positioned in four belts: between the upper and lower belts of palmettos there are 15 'female' heads and under it are 6 pairs of oppositely positioned ram heads separated by 6 lion heads. The female heads are full face and allude to a goddess which, because of the lion heads can be defined as a hypostasis of Bendida.

The number of goddesses makes a very strong impression: they are 15. This number allows (along with a number of other data) to perceive the echo of one of the ancient calendars in Thrace because the number of 15 in this particular case probably corresponds to the number of weeks in the so-called nundial year. The nundial calendar had been related to a year consisting of four months, each of thirty days. Three such years formed a solar year (3x4x30 = 360 + 5 intercalary days = 365), the week consisting of 8 days.

Protome of Pegasus from a high-horned rhyton
Gold. Accidental finding, the village of
Vazovo (District of Razgrad); height
14.8 cm, weight 475.8 g.
Before 339 BC?
The horn of the rhyton is missing.
On the protome the winged Pegasus

is presented galloping with a tall
horn between its ears, with broad
wings and its nozzle is expressively
rendered. Wings are well shaped but
the elements of the horse harness
have obviously been hammered out
additionally and rather schematically,
by notches of dots.

Thracian King's crown of laurels
Gold. Mogilanska Mogila, town of
Vratsa; diameter 24 cm, weight 205 g.
Third quarter of the 4th century BC.
It was found in the so-called grave No.
2, a burial chamber with dimensions
11x4 m where in its eastern end
two horses are laid together with the
chariot and apart of them there is the
skeleton of another horse. Near the
latter archaeologists have found the
remains of a man with a spear and at a
distance of about 3.5 m, in the western

part of the chamber lies the skeleton of
a 'young man', his face turned towards
the ground and to whom the crown
belonged. Its branches and leaves are
realistically rendered: one can see the
veins of the leaves, while from the
branches stalks come out on which
ball-shaped fruits are affixed. The
rhyton is identical with the one from
the Rozovets treasure dated, in most
general terms, from the first half of the
4th century BC.

Thracian breast-plates

1. Gold breast-plate (length 13.8 cm, 19.60 g) from Banova Mogila near the village Douvanliy, with an image of a lion (according to some authors it is the image of a dog), with a drooping head, prolonged ears, long nose, bulging cheeks with four folds each, long tail and four-fingered paws.
Third quarter of the 5th century BC.

2. Gold breast-plate (length 25.9 cm, weight 65.5 g) from Moushovitsa Mogila of the Odryses' royal necropolis near the village Douvanliy, of irregular shape (something between ellipse and rhomb) and a decoration of nightingales.
Second half of the 4th century BC.

3. Two gold breast-plates (a little one, 17.5 cm long, weighing 28 g, and a big one, 38.5 cm long, weighing 86.8 g) with a decoration of pearls and other

elements, from the Golyamata (Big) Mogila of the Odryses' royal necropolis near the village Douvanliy.
Around the middle of the 5th century BC.

4. Gold breast-plate from the village Sakalitsa, District of Yambol (length 16.1 cm, weight 6.79 g) with a decoration of pearls, zigzag, fishbone and schematically rendered trees.
4th century BC.

In Europe, breast-plates were found for the first time in Mycenaean tombs and are known from Fore Asia, Anatolia and Etruscan lands. The earliest so far specimen form Thrace is the one found at Moushovitsa Mogila. In the period from 6th through 4th century BC, Thracian breast-plates represent the latest European manifestation of this type of monuments and testify to one of the basic royal attributes.

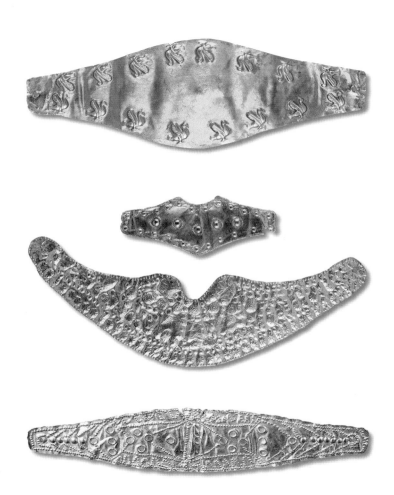

Thracian solid fold ring
Gold. Golyamata Mogila of the
Odryses' royal necropolis near
Douvanliy; diameter 2.6 cm, weight
13.75 g.
Around the middle of the 5th
century BC
The ring from the Golyamata Mogila

barrow was found together with two
pectorals (breast-plates) some distance
away from the remains of a member
of the Odryses' royal family buried by
incineration. It belonged to Scythodoc
as can be seen from the inscription in
Greek in dative: ΣΚΥΘΟΔΟΚΟ („To
Scythodoc").

Gold ring
Gold. Village Ezerovo (District of Plovdiv); diameter 2.7 cm, weight 31.3 g. 5th century BC.
The ring from Ezerovo has an inscription in Thracian language but the letters are ancient Greek:
ΡΟΛΙΣΤΕΝΕΑΣΝ / ΕΡΕΝΕΑΤΙΛ / ΤΕΑΝΗΣΚΟΑ / ΡΑΖΕΑΔΟΜ / ΕΑΝΤΙΛΕΖΥ / ΠΤΑΜΙ-

ΗΕ / ΡΑΖΗΛΤΑ. This text has not been translated for sure. The data supplied by Herodotos (5.5) on the burial practices of Thracians "who live above the Krestons" has permitted to accept provisionally that the ring had belonged to Tiltea who had been selected to die together with her husband Rol.

Gold mask-phial

Gold. Mogila Svetitsa in the 'Valley of Thracian Kings', 673 g.
4th century BC?

This massive gold mask has no parallels even among Mycenaean gold death masks of the late Bronze Age. It is made not from thin gold folio but from thick gold sheet metal. It is shaped like phial, which makes it a unique item of this kind.

The assumptions that the rigorous face with a heavy curly beard and hair belongs to the founder of the Odryses' kingdom Teres I is beneath criticism. Chronologically, the mask-phial is closest to the beardless Phoenician gold masks from 5th – 4th century

BC kept in the Louvre. This particular mask was found complete with the accoutrements of a heavily armed horseman with bronze armor and sensational iron components: collar, sleeves, a midriff-plate, protective belt for the lower part of the body, fastening elements and a multitude of items knitted of rings (it might be the earliest known to us knitted chain-mails, currently considered to be a medieval patent).

All such findings raise quite a lot of questions, which can be solved only after a publication is made that is to meet the contemporary research and scientific criteria.

CONSIDERABLE THRACIAN TREASURES FOUND IN BULGARIAN LANDS (6TH TO 3RD CENTURIES BC)

1. The village Douvanliy (District of Plovdiv): treasure items from Moushovitsa Mogila, Koukova Mogila, Golyamata Mogila, Bashova Mogila and Arabadzhi Mogila; dated the end of the 6th till the first decades of the 4th century BC.

2. The village Garchinovo (District of Shoumen): an accidental finding of a matrix dated the 6th – 5th centuries BC.

3. The village Skrebatno (District of Blagoevgrad): a set of gold objects dated the 6th – 5th centuries BC.

4. The village Lovets (District of Stara Zagora): an accidental finding dated the 6th or the beginning of the 5th century BC.

5. The village Daskal Atanasovo (District of Stara Zagora): an accidental finding consisting of three gold phials dated the 5th century BC.

6. The village Dalboki (District of Stara Zagora): treasure items in a funeral dated the 5th century BC.

7. The village Boukyovtsi (District of Oryakhovo): two mixed treasures containing items from the Kingdom of Odryses dated the end of the 5th – the beginning of the 4th centuries BC.

8. The village Tvarditsa (District of Blagoevgrad): treasure items in a funeral dated the third quarter of the 5th century BC.

9. The village Kaloyanovo (District of Plovdiv): treasure items, gold breast-plate from a barrow necropolis dated the 5th – 4th centuries BC.

10. The village Mezek (District of Svilengrad): barrow necropolis with treasure items found at the Srednata Mogila, Maltepe and the Malkata Mogila; dated the end of the 5th and the beginning of the 3rd centuries BC.

11. The village Brezovo (District of Plovdiv): treasure items in a funeral dated the end of the 5th – the beginning of the 4th century BC.

12. The village Rogozen (District of Vratsa): a mixed treasure dated the end of the 5th century BC until 340-339 BC, when Phillip II the Macedon plundered and then lost part of the Odryses' royal treasury.

13. The barrow Ryazana Mogila (District of Blagoevgrad): a treasure find dated the end of the 5th – the first half of the 4th centuries BC.

14. The village Radyuvene (district of Lovech): a large mixed treasure containing phials from the Odryses' Kingdom dated the end of the 4th century BC.

15. The village Alexandrovo (District of Lovech): a mixed treasure dated the 4th century BC containing items from the Odryses' Kingdom.

16. The village Borovo (District of Rousse): a treasure dated from the reign of King Kotys I (around 383 - 360 BC).

17. The village Branichevo (District of Shoumen): a funeral with treasure items dated the 4th century BC, containing also a phial belonging to the Odryses' King Amadok I or Amadok II.

18. Vladinya: a treasure dated the 4th century BC.

19. Town of Varbitsa (District of Preslav): treasure items of Odryses' Kingdom origin, dated the 4th century BC.

20. The village Letnitsa (District of Lovech): a treasure from the reign of King Kotys I and his son Kerseblept (dated the second quarter of the 4th century BC)

21. Town of Strelcha (Region of Panagyurishte): remains from objects and a scyphos in a barrow funeral dated the 4th century BC.

22. The village Sveshtari (District of Razgrad): an accidental find of silver nose-plate dated the 4th century BC.

23. The village Dolna Koznitsa (District of Kyustendil): silver applications dated the 4th century BC.

24. Town of Chirpan (Region of Stara Zagora): a gold ring with a 'labris' dated the 4th century BC.

25. The village Gradnitsa: an accidental finding of a phial dated the 4th century BC.

26. The village Kapinovo (District of Veliko Tarnovo): a funeral with treasure items dated the second half of the 4th century BC.

27. The Mogilanska Mogila near the town of Vratsa: treasure items dated the 4th century BC; among them objects were found from the Odryses' royal treasury.

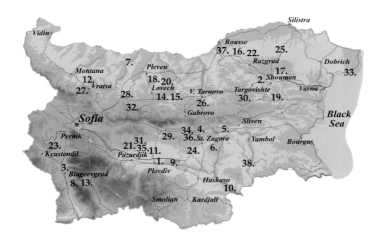

28. Town of Loukovit: a mixed treasure dated the 4th century BC containing objects from the Odryses' Kingdom.

29. The village Rozovets (District of Karlovo): funeral treasure items and a gold wreath dated the second half of the 4th century BC.

30. The village Kralevo (District of Targovishte): a treasure dated the second half of the 4th century BC.

31. Town of Panagyurishte (Region of Pazardzhik): treasure items from funerals and a gold treasure dated the second half of the 4th – the beginning of the 3rd centuries BC.

32. Teteven: phials from a funeral dated the second half of the 4th century BC.

33. Town of Kavarna: a gold wreath from a funeral, dated the last quarter of the 4th century BC.

34. 'The Valley of Thracian Kings' (District of Kazanlak): treasure items found at: Ostrousha Mogila, a funeral-cult complex built in the second half of the 4th century BC, the greater part of the treasure probably plundered in the 4th century AD; Sineva Mogila, treasure items dated the 4th century BC; Malkata Mogila, unspoiled barrow tomb dated the 4th – the beginning of the 3rd centuries BC; Sashova Mogila, unspoiled barrow complex dated the 3rd -2nd centuries BC; Bineva, Matildina, Tsvyatkova and Zareva Mogila dated the second half of the 4th – 3rd centuries BC.

35. The village Starosel (District of Hissar): Thracian cult complex, treasure items found there dated the second half of the 4th – the beginning of the 3rd centuries BC.

36. Seuthopolis (District of Kazanlak): items found at barrow funeral dated the end of the 4th – the beginning of the 3rd centuries BC; The Kazanlak Tomb: silver little pitcher found in the backfill of the barrow, dated the second half of the 4th century BC.

37. The village Koprivets (District of Rousse): gold decorations from a funeral dated the end of the 4th – the beginning of the 3rd century BC.

38. The village Zlatinitsa (District of Bolyarovo): treasure items from a barrow funeral dated the 4th century BC.

Many more yet unpublished finds are known to experts, hundreds of treasure items, which have been entered the museums' inventories marked in most general terms by the locality they had been found or filed as "place of origin unknown' and so on…

BULGARIA
THE LAND OF TREASURES

with 108 colour illustrations

Text: Atanas Orachev, Antoniy Handjiyski
Photos: Vyara Kandjeva,
Antoniy Handjiyski,
Rosen Kolev
Dessin: Antoniy Handjiyski
English translation: Vladimir Pomakov
Editor of the Bulgarian text: Vyara Kandjeva
Prepress: Geo Kovatchev

BORINA Publishing House
E-mail: borina@borina.com
www.borina.com

ISBN 954-500-164-X

Printed in the Czech Republic